And The *I's* Have it

Eight steps to developing a closer relationship with God

Dr. Shenequa C. Miller

And The *I's* Have it
EIGHT STEPS TO DEVELOPING A CLOSER RELATIONSHIP WITH GOD
By Dr. Shenequa C. Miller

Copyright 2024
Dr. Shenequa C. Miller

No part of this book may be reproduced, distributed or transmitted in any form by any means, graphics, electronics, or mechanical, including photocopy, recording, taping, or by any information storage or retrieval system, without permission in writing from the publisher or without the express written consent of the author, except in the case of reprints in the context of reviews, quotes or references.

Printed in the United States of America

ISBN: 979-8-218-47017-3

The Phoenix Firm, LLC
Publishing Division
Texas

Unless otherwise specified, Scripture Verses are taken from the following:

King James Version. (1769). Holy Bible. Cambridge University Press.

New King James Version. (1982). Holy Bible. Thomas Nelson.

New International Version. (2011). Holy Bible. Zondervan.

English Standard Version. (2001). Holy Bible. Crossway.

New Living Translation. (1996). Holy Bible. Tyndale House Publishers.

Photographer Anthony Lyles, Chapters 1, 2, 5 and Conclusion.

All photos used granted subjects permission for purposes of printing.

Dedication

I attribute all recognition and success of this book to my Lord and Savior, Jesus Christ.

Without Jesus in my life, there would not be a book and most importantly, no narrative to share.

This book is dedicated to my maternal grandmother Willie Mae Cook, paternal grandparents Altha Lee and Charles Edward Easley, my parents Mae Ella Cook and James Charles Easley. All who have passed and would have offered encouragement, embraced my vision, and joyously commemorated the day I exclaimed, "I've finished my first book!"

To my wonderful husband of 32 years Reggie, our children Jasmine, Reggie Jr., Adrian, and Jordan, our grandchildren Ava and Aubrey, and my closest friends (you know who you are), I express my gratitude.

I will never be able to thank you enough.

Preface

More than a decade ago, I made a promise to myself, I would author a book. It sounded straightforward enough—find an attention-grabbing title, design an appealing cover, share my personal experiences and challenges, and voila! Like magic, a New York Times bestseller, right? If only the process of writing a book were that simple. Nevertheless, I persevered, jotting down words here and there, year after year to create a quality product for others to enjoy. Today, what you hold in your hands or have downloaded onto your preferred device, is a complete culmination of that effort. May the words that God has inspired me to share within these pages provide you with the encouragement you need to move from where you are today, to where you are destined to be. Amen.

Table of Contents

Introduction	6
Chapter 1: Introspection	11
Chapter 2: Incorporate Prayer	23
Chapter 3: Increase Scripture Study	39
Chapter 4: Invoke Gratitude	51
Chapter 5: Inner Transformation	59
Chapter 6: Integrate Community	71
Chapter 7: Invest in Service	83
Chapter 8: Ignite Worship	92
Conclusion	105
Prayer	107

Introduction

Have you ever felt like you were drifting further away from God with each passing day - like your life is lacking something, and wonder about God's purposes for you? Have you ever felt tired of always setting New Year resolutions to get closer to God, yet do not make satisfactory progress by the end of the year; and wish to end this by following a practical guide that works?

If you have answered YES, you will find this book helpful!

It is every believer's wish to live in the reality of James 4:8 (NIV), which says *"Come near to God and He will come near to you..."*

However, our sinful nature gets in the way (better known as free will), just as Paul describes in Romans 7:15-20 (NIV), *"I do not understand what I do. For what I want to do I do not do, but what I hate I do. And if I do what I do not want to do, I agree that the law is good. As it is, it is no longer I who does it, but it is sin living in me. For I know that good itself does not dwell in me, that is, in my sinful nature. For I have the desire to do what is good, but I cannot carry it out. I do not do the good I want to do, but the evil I do not want to do—this I keep doing. Now if I do what I do not want to do, it is no longer I who does it, but it is sin living in me that does it."*

And even as we get closer to God, our soul still hungers for God's presence just as the Psalmist describes it in Psalm 42:1-2 (NIV): *"As the deer pants for streams of water, so my soul pants for you, my God. My soul thirsts for God, for the living God. When can I go and meet with God?"* and Psalm 63:1 (NIV) *"You, God, are my God, earnestly I seek you; I thirst for you, my whole being longs for you, in a dry and parched land where there is no water."*

Indeed, regardless of your relationship with God, there is no denying that we all want to have a deeper connection with Him. We wish God could give a testimony about us as "A man or woman after

God's own heart" as Samuel described David to King Saul. The million-dollar question remains, How or is that even possible?

Well, for starters, it is important to appreciate the fact that developing a strong relationship with God (the type described in some of the verses above) is not something that happens overnight but is a lifelong journey of faith, prayer, obedience, and love. However, it is completely possible to be so connected to God that you make His glory and presence manifest in everywhere you go and in everything you do. All you need is to seek Him with all your heart, as Jeremiah 29:13 (NIV) described: *"You will seek me and find me when you seek me with all your heart."*

Fortunately, by design, this book contains eight practical steps you can apply in your walk of faith to get to know Him more, experience His presence, and see His power manifest in your life. In the end, you will live true to the promises made in Matthew 6:33 (NIV) *"But seek first his kingdom and his righteousness, and all these things will be given to you as well."* And Proverbs 3:5-6 (NIV): *"Trust in the Lord with all your heart and lean not on your own understanding; in all your ways submit to him, and he will make your paths straight."*

More precisely, you will learn:
- The place of introspection in building your daily walk with Christ – why it is a critical first step in an ongoing process called life.

- How to incorporate prayer in your Christian walk.

- Why and how to increase your scripture study.

- Why invoking gratitude will move you closer to a life of knowing Him.

- How to go through an inner transformation journey for His glory.

- The place of integrating community in your walk with God.

- How investing in service will make you a better Christian – and how to go about it.

- How to ignite worship in your every moment walk with Christ.

- And so much more!

By following this book's steps, you can intentionally and purposefully build a closer relationship with God! Even if you have failed many times in the past, or even felt like an imposter in the Kingdom of God, you are equipped and, on your way, to try again. This book will prove inspiring and thought-provoking as you move forward this time, with success.

You are not alone in your journey of faith. I have been through many struggles and challenges in my life, and I want to share with you how God has helped me overcome them all. In this book, you will find some of my personal stories that illustrate how God's grace and love have transformed me. I hope that by reading them, you will feel closer to God and inspired to trust Him more than ever before.

Let us begin!

DR. SHENEQUA C. MILLER

And The I's Have It

EIGHT STEPS TO DEVELOPING A CLOSER RELATIONSHIP WITH GOD

Chapter 1: Introspection

Before you can make any changes in your walk with Christ, you will first need to understand where you are and your current relationship with God. That is why the first step in our journey to building a closer relationship with God is about introspection.

1 Corinthians 11:28 (NIV), says, *"Everyone ought to examine themselves...."*

While the context was in line with the Lord's Supper, the truth is that self-examination should be something we all do as Christians on an ongoing basis - not just when we are about to take Holy Communion. It is through self-introspection that we can reflect on our thoughts, feelings, and actions (actions and inactions) and assess areas where we can grow spiritually and align them with God's will. It is a time of truth, to face our fears and lean on God for understanding and not that of our own.

Lamentations 3:40 (NIV), tells us, *"Let us examine our ways and evaluate them, and let us return to the Lord..."*

This verse suggests the importance of introspection by examining our ways and reflecting on our actions to ensure that they align with God's will. Although the specific word "introspection" might not be mentioned, the act of self-examination is encouraged in this passage.

Introspection is a valuable tool for spiritual growth because it allows us as believers to identify areas of strength, weakness, growth, and areas where we may need to seek forgiveness or make changes. Through introspection, we can evaluate our attitudes, motives, and behaviors, and assess what aligns with the teachings of God. It is a true examination as to who we really are versus just who we want others to believe we are.

By engaging in introspection, we can recognize areas of spiritual growth, identify barriers that hinder our relationship with God, and again, make necessary adjustments to align ourselves more closely with God's will. It allows for greater self-awareness and helps us identify areas where we need to surrender our will to God's plan. We learn that our lives are not our own, but The Lord's.

We can also develop a stronger sense of gratitude and appreciation for God's blessings in our lives. It allows us to acknowledge and reflect on how God has been present, guiding, shaping our spiritual journey, and literally going before us everywhere we go.

While self-reflection is crucial for discovery, growth, and healing, it should be accompanied by reliance on God's grace and guidance rather than solely relying on personal efforts. It is in this humble recognition of our limitations and dependence on God that true growth and transformation can and will occur, Amen.

When approached with sincerity and a willingness to change, introspection can be a powerful tool for developing a closer relationship with God. It helps us to seek His guidance, align our thoughts and actions with His will, and continually grow in our faith. But most importantly, how can we Biblically apply self-examination? Here are some ideas:

Pray for guidance and wisdom!

Before you start introspecting, ask God to help you see yourself as He sees you, and to reveal anything that He wants you to know or change. This is such a powerful testament to the power of looking within oneself with honesty and truth. Trust that He will speak to you through your thoughts, feelings, and dreams, that He will show you His love and grace.

Just like the song in Psalm 139:23-2, "*Search through me, O God, and know my heart; Search me and know my anxious thoughts. See if there is any offensive way in me and lead me in the way of eternity."* This shows us that self-examination is not something we do on our own but with God's help. We ask Him to search our hearts and reveal anything that is not pleasing to Him. If we are honest with ourselves while doing this, we often find many things we do are not pleasing to us as well. We also ask Him to guide us in the right direction, which leads to peace on earth and an ultimate eternal life with Him.

Ask yourself a few questions.

2 Corinthians 13:5 says, *"Examine yourself to see if you are in the faith; Examine yourself. Do you not see that Christ Jesus is in you—unless, of course, you fail the test?"*

This passage reminds us that self-examination involves not only our feelings and motivations but also our beliefs and actions. We need to find out if we are truly living according to the word of God and if Christ lives in us as per Galatians 2:20 (NIV): *"I have been crucified with Christ and I no longer live, but Christ lives in me. The life I now live in the body, I live by faith in the Son of God, who loved me and gave himself for me."*

When we realize that we are not in the faith, we need to repent and return to God. To help you figure out this, here are some prompts to guide your self-examination. The next series of questions may take a while to complete. Do not get discouraged; yet be encouraged to take your time. Remember that self-introspection is a personal and ongoing process. Feel free to adapt these prompts to suit your unique journey and relationship with God. Most importantly, be patient with yourself and use journaling as a tool to explore your relationship with God and work toward breakthroughs in your spiritual life.

Accountability and Support: Do you have a support system or accountability partner in your spiritual journey? How might this type of relationship help you grow closer to God?

Biblical Examples: Consider the stories of biblical figures like Joseph, Esther, or Paul, who faced challenges and setbacks but realized they were part of God's greater plan. What lessons can you draw from their experiences?

Describe Your Current Spiritual Practices: Detail your current habits and practices related to your faith and spirituality. What do you regularly do to nurture your relationship with God?

Embracing Change: Explore your attitude toward change and transitions in life. How can you embrace change as a potential part of God's plan rather than resisting it?

Examine Expectations: What expectations do you have regarding your relationship with God? Are these expectations attainable or realistic? Be reminded not to put too much pressure on yourself.

Goals and Intentions: What are your spiritual goals and intentions? Where do you see yourself in your relationship with God in the future?

God's Faithfulness: Reflect on times when you felt God's presence or experienced His faithfulness during difficult circumstances. How did these experiences reveal His greater plan for you?

Gratitude for God's Plan: List things you are grateful for that have been a part of God's plan for your life. Express thankfulness for both the big and small blessings.

Journal a Letter to Your Future Self: Write a letter to your future self, expressing your hopes and aspirations for how God's plan will continue to unfold in your life.

Overcoming Challenges: Recall significant challenges you have faced and how they shaped your character or led you to new opportunities. Did these challenges align with God's plan for your growth?

Prayer for Guidance: Write a prayer asking God to reveal His greater plan for your life. Pour out your desires and seek His guidance.

Reflect on Past Events: Can you recall instances in your life where things did not go according to your plan but turned out better in the end? Write about these experiences and how they might relate to God's greater plan.

Seeking Guidance: Are there specific areas where you feel you need guidance or mentorship in your spiritual journey? Who could you turn to for support?

Serving Others: Write about the times when serving or helping others brought a sense of fulfillment. How might serving others align with God's greater purpose for your life?

Surrendering Control: Explore your willingness (or unwillingness) to surrender control to God. Are there areas in your life where you struggle to let go and trust His plan?

Write a Letter to God: Consider writing a letter to God, expressing your feelings, struggles, and desires in your own words.

Respond to what you discover.

After you finish introspecting, do not just leave it there. Act based on what you learned about yourself and God. Hebrews 4:12 (NIV) says, *"For the word of God is alive and active. Sharper than any double-edged sword, it penetrates even to dividing soul and spirit, joints and marrow; it judges the thoughts and attitudes of the heart."* This verse tells us that God's Word is an excellent tool for self-examination. It is powerful and effective, able to reveal our innermost thoughts and attitudes. He also judges them according to His perfect and holy standards. We need to read and study God's Word regularly to know what to do with whatever we have discovered through introspection.

Also, James 1:22-25 teaches us the importance of self-examination. It says *"Do not merely listen to the word, and so deceive yourselves. Do what it says. Anyone who listens to the word but does not do what it says is like someone who looks at his face in a mirror and, after looking at himself, goes away and immediately forgets what he looks like. But whoever looks intently into the perfect law that gives freedom and continues in it—not forgetting what they have heard but doing it—they will be blessed in what they do."* This verse challenges us to examine our lives and see if we are living according to God's will. It encourages us to study and apply God's Word, the source of true freedom and blessings. As stated, several times, self-examination is not easy, but it is necessary for spiritual growth and development.

Introspection is a very powerful tool that can help you get closer to God and truly understand who you are. By practicing it regularly, you can deepen your self-awareness, improve your self-control, strengthen your relationship with God, know when you are in sin, hear when God is speaking, and live a more meaningful and fulfilling life.

My Story:

At one time during my early 20's, I was completely determined to control every aspect of my life. Not just some areas of my life, every single aspect of it. Though I believed in God, I also struggled to fully trust God and often found myself burdened with worry and anxiety time after time again.

One day, after a long workout, I came across a quote in a magazine that said, "To trust God is to let go of control." These words deeply resonated with me, and I started to evaluate my faith and relationship with God. How could I say I trust God, still worry, and have anxiety at times? I knew something was not right and wanted to figure it out. Realizing that my worry and anxiety were hindering my spiritual growth, I embarked on a journey of introspection.

The journey did not start out perfectly, not even a little bit. However, I forced myself to make time with God a priority versus using "extra" time to spend with Him. I began by setting aside quiet moments each day, seeking solitude for self-reflection and prayer. In these moments, I honestly examined my thoughts, fears, denials, and insecurities. I discovered that my need for control stemmed from a fear of the unknown and a lack of trust in God's plan for my life. Admitting this was not easy, but it was necessary for me to grow and move forward. In all honesty, the process of admitting I really did not have the faith in God that I thought I had, made me feel like a failure.

Throughout the process, I identified my patterns of worry and anxiety and recognized the amount of time wasted each day, which was quite disturbing to me. As I delved deeper into my introspective journey, I started to realize that my desire for control was limiting my ability to experience true peace and joy as well. I could recognize it more because I was really paying attention and looking for commonalities and patterns.

With each dedicated prayer and reflective time with God, I found myself gradually releasing my grip on controlling every outcome and instead, surrendering to God's guidance. I began to trust that God's plan was far greater than anything I could conceive or orchestrate on my own. As painful as it was, I realized I was not the author of my own fate.

I was amazed that through introspection, I was able to reveal the areas I lacked faith and how I resisted God in His efforts to lead as the head of my life. I acknowledged my fears and doubts, and through heartfelt prayers, I asked God to help strengthen my faith and restore trust in myself through Him.

As I started to be a little more patient in my decision-making and wait on God's voice, I started to recognize the blessings and moments of divine guidance that I had previously overlooked. Again, I was able to recognize it more because I was very intentional in looking for patterns in my routines and daily tasks. By acknowledging and appreciating these instances, my trust in God deepened more than I could have ever imagined. I realized that introspection was not only about examining my faults but also about recognizing God's faithfulness and provision in my life throughout it all.

Through my renewed and anchored trust in God, I experienced a sense of freedom and peace that I had never felt before. I no longer felt the need to control every single little detail of my life, but instead, I surrendered my worries to God, knowing that He had a perfect plan for me. A comfort I had never felt before, an inner peace was with me like nothing I had ever felt before. That was my assurance, I was within God's will.

My introspective journey completely transformed my relationship with God. By trusting in His loving guidance, I discovered new opportunities, witnessed miracles, and experienced the joy of walking hand in hand with my Creator, Hallelujah! Through introspection, I not only deepened my trust in God but also cultivated a greater sense of gratitude for His presence in my life.

Soon I found myself growing more dependent and reliant on God's wisdom and guidance. Rather than relying solely on my own understanding, I sought God's perspective and surrendered my fears and doubts all to Him. My talk began to match my walk "in" Christ and not on my own accord. I was not in control of my life, yet I was finally in control of my life (if that makes sense).

Working through introspection also allowed me to recognize and address areas where I needed to let go of past hurts and forgive those who had wronged me. This was so hard; a true process that took a lot of time going on an emotional rollercoaster with feelings of anger, disappointment, sadness, tears, peace and finally calmness. However, through prayer and reflection, I found healing and the strength to extend forgiveness; experiencing the freedom that comes from releasing the burdens of resentment. I did not go back to rebuild broken relationships but allowed myself time to understand that people come in and out of my life for seasons unknown by me, but known by my Father in Heaven, Amen.

I like to call my experience a "transformative power of introspection." I became a living testament to the power of trust in God. My newfound trust radiated to those around me, in and outside of my home. People knew and could see something different about me and in me that was almost indescribable. This "glow" was inspiring others to embark on their introspective journey and deepen their relationship with God right along with me.

My story is a reminder that introspection, coupled with trust in God, can lead to personal growth, increased faith, and a closer relationship with Jesus Christ. Introspection is a tool we can use to open our hearts and minds to God's work within us, allowing Him to transform us from the inside out, which is literally amazing to experience and share. It is truly an honor to allow God to be your safety net and guide through life on earth, Amen.

The other thing you need to do is to incorporate prayer into your everyday life. Let us learn more about that next.

Your Story:

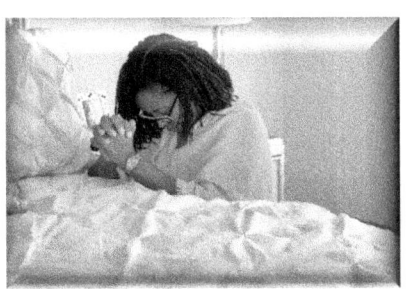

Chapter 2: Incorporate Prayer

Apostle Paul wrote in his first letter to the Thessalonians in chapter 5 verse 17 he told them to "Pray without ceasing..."

Through prayer, we can make our supplications before the Lord, confess our sins, intercede for others, commune with God, receive healing and restoration, build our faith and trust in God, transform our character, praise, worship and so much more.

This is something that all of us as believers ought to do, even when it does not feel like our prayers are getting what we often refer to as "breakthroughs". Our lifestyle must be characterized by a consistent and ongoing attitude of prayer, where we turn to God during all times – whether during times of joy, sorrow, or challenges in life. Let us repeat that again, together: Our lifestyle must be characterized by a consistent and ongoing attitude of prayer, where we turn to God during all times – whether during times of joy, sorrow, or challenges in life.

We should not give up even when we struggle to find the right words to say or feel that our prayers are ineffective or simply just not good enough. Even Jesus told his disciples in Luke 18: 1 a parable to show them to always pray and not give up.

In 1 Thessalonians 5:16-18, *"Rejoice always, pray without ceasing, give thanks in all circumstances; for this is the will of God in Christ Jesus for you,"* Paul encourages all the believers in Thessalonica, who were facing persecution and hardship to rejoice always, pray without ceasing, and give thanks in all circumstances, for this is the will of God. This verse encourages believers to maintain a continual and genuine attitude of prayer, recognizing its significance in their relationship with God.

We should have it in our hearts to pray without ceasing and be grateful for the opportunity to pray. But how can we pray without ceasing? Does it mean blocking out everything else and spending all your time on your knees? Does it mean we do not have faith at all because we continue to pray and ask God, not genuinely believing our prayers will be heard and answered in God's timing? Not at all!

Praying without ceasing has more to do with the attitude of your heart than the posture of your body. This means that you need to constantly be aware of God's presence, always ready to communicate with Him, always willing to hear His voice, and always obedient to His will. As you can see, the emphasis is on "always" and not during times of distress, or magnificent moments.

David challenges us Christians on how to pray without ceasing in Psalm 34:1, where he says, "*I will bless the Lord at all times; his praise shall continually be in my mouth.*" He goes further ahead in Psalm 55:17, where he says, "*Evening and morning and at noon I utter my complaint and moan, and he hears my voice.*" It is no wonder there is a testimony that David was a man after God's heart!

You can incorporate prayer in your life by being more intentional with the strategies listed below.

Starting your day with prayer

Before you do anything else, dedicate your day to God and ask Him to guide, protect, and use you for His glory. As David shared his morning prayer in Psalms 5:3, "*In the morning, Lord, you hear my voice; in the morning I lay my requests before you and wait expectantly.*" David has a relationship with God that was incredibly special. His prayers were beautiful and meaningful; a true testament to his love for God. Beginning your day with prayer is a powerful way to connect with God and align your heart with His will.

Pray throughout the day.

As you go about your daily activities, remember the words in Ephesians 6:18: It reads, "*Pray in the Spirit on all occasions with all kinds of prayers and requests. With this in mind, be alert and always keep on praying for all the Lord's people.*" Keep a constant conversation with God where you thank Him for His blessings, ask Him for His help, confess your sins, intercede for others, praise Him for His attributes, and worship Him for His works. Philippians 4:6 (NIV) goes ahead and adds "*Do not be anxious about anything, but in every situation, by prayer and petition, with thanksgiving, present your requests to God.*" This means there are countless opportunities to pray at any time or place.

End your day with prayer.

Psalm 4:8 says, "*In peace, I will both lie down and sleep; for you alone, O Lord, make me dwell in safety.*" Before you go to sleep, review your day with God and thank Him for His faithfulness, grace, and mercy. Ask Him to forgive you for any sins you committed (sins of commission and omission) and give you peace and rest throughout the night. We sometimes become so busy, we forget each sin we have committed throughout the day. Therefore, be reminded of the importance of asking for forgiveness of sins you are able to remember and those you may have forgotten.

Pray according to God's Word.

One of the best ways to pray without ceasing is to pray according to God's Word. The Bible is full of prayers that we can use as models, such as the Lord's Prayer (Matthew 6:9-13), the Psalms (Psalm 23), and the prayers of Jesus (John 17). We can also use God's promises, commands, and character as guides for our prayers. John 15:7 says, "*If you abide in me, and my words abide in you, ask whatever you wish, and it will be done for you.*" Just knowing the power in the Scriptures, we are a blessed people indeed.

Pray in the Spirit.

Another way to pray without ceasing is to pray in the Spirit, as Romans 8:26-27 says, "*Likewise the Spirit helps us in our weakness. For we do not know what to pray for as we ought, but the Spirit himself intercedes for us with groanings too deep for words. And he who searches hearts knows what the mind of the Spirit is because the Spirit intercedes for the saints according to the will of God.*" This means that we rely on the Holy Spirit to help us pray according to God's will, even when we do not know what to say or how to say it. It is not by our prowess or experience in prayer but by the spirit that we commune with God in prayer. Therefore, even if you do not pray in a flowery style like your friend or that sibling from your fellowship, what matters is to let yourself go – let the need to control the prayer go and let the spirit of God take over.

Pray with others.

We are not meant to pray alone all the time but as part of a community of believers who support each other and share each other's burdens. Matthew 18:19-20 says, "*Again I say to you, if two of you agree on earth about anything they ask, it will be done for them by my Father in heaven. For where two or three are gathered in my name, there am I among them.*" This guides us Christians to pray with our family members, friends, church members, or anyone who needs prayer.

Just to recap, Prayer is one of the most essential practices a true Christian can engage in. It is how we connect with God, give thanks, acknowledge our transgressions, seek His direction, and intercede on behalf of others. Prayer provides a way in which we experience God's presence, strength, and calm in our lives.

Here are some verses that highlight the importance of prayer:

Matthew 6:9-13: The Lord's Prayer, taught by Jesus Himself, is a model for incorporating prayer into our lives. It outlines the essential elements of prayer, including acknowledging and honoring God, seeking His will, and asking for provision, forgiveness, and guidance.

Philippians 4:6-7: *"Do not be anxious about anything, but in everything by prayer and supplication with thanksgiving let your requests be made known to God. And the peace of God, which surpasses all understanding, will guard your hearts and your minds in Christ Jesus."* This verse encourages believers to bring their concerns, worries, and requests to God in prayer, with an attitude of thanksgiving, knowing that He cares for them.

Mark 11:24: "Therefore I tell you, whatever you ask in prayer, believe that you have received it, and it will be yours." God has provided the formula for us to best communicate with Him, as well as the outcome. What a privilege to know Jesus Christ! Amen.

The next few strategies are to help you incorporate prayer into your life and get closer to God:

Set Aside Dedicated Time: Schedule specific times for prayer during your day or week. Create a sacred space where you can retreat and focus solely on your connection with God. Jesus supports this concept of a dedicated prayer area in Matthew 6:6 (NIV): *"But when you pray, go into your room, close the door, and pray to your unseen Father. Then your father, who sees what is done in secret, will reward you."* Secret is equivalent to private and intimate time with God.

Engage in Different Forms of Prayer: Explore various forms of prayer such as adoration, confession, thanksgiving, and supplication (ACTS). Include silent contemplation, intercessory prayer for others, and listening prayer to hear God's voice. The ACTS model of prayer is a helpful framework that guides individuals through different forms of prayer: Adoration, Confession, Thanksgiving, and Supplication. Here are some Bible verses and concepts related to each aspect of ACTS, as well as additional forms of prayer like silent contemplation, intercessory prayer, and listening prayer:

Adoration (Worship)

Psalm 95:6 (NIV): *"Come, let us bow down in worship, let us kneel before the Lord our Maker."*

Revelation 4:11 (NIV): *"You are worthy, our Lord and God, to receive glory and honor and power, for you created all things, and by your will, they were created and have their being."*

Adoration involves praising God for who He is, acknowledging His greatness, and expressing reverence and awe in His presence.

Confession (Repentance)

1 John 1:9 (NIV): *"If we confess our sins, he is faithful and just and will forgive us our sins and purify us from all unrighteousness."*

Psalm 32:5 (NIV): *"Then I acknowledged my sin to you and did not cover up my iniquity. I said, 'I will confess my transgressions to the Lord.' And you forgave the guilt of my sin."*

Confession involves acknowledging and repenting of sins, seeking God's forgiveness, and experiencing spiritual cleansing.

Thanksgiving (Gratitude)

1 Thessalonians 5:18 (NIV): *"Give thanks in all circumstances; for this is God's will for you in Christ Jesus."*

Psalm 107:1 (NIV): *"Give thanks to the Lord, for he is good; his love endures forever."*

Thanksgiving involves expressing gratitude to God for His blessings, provisions, and the goodness He has shown in our lives.

Supplication (Petition)

Philippians 4:6-7 (NIV): *"Do not be anxious about anything, but in every situation, by prayer and petition, with thanksgiving, present your requests to God. And the peace of God, which transcends all understanding, will guard your hearts and your minds in Christ Jesus."*

James 5:16 (NIV): *"Therefore confess your sins to each other and pray for each other so that you may be healed. The prayer of a righteous person is powerful and effective."*

Supplication involves bringing our specific requests, needs, and concerns before God in prayer, both for ourselves and for others.

Additional Forms of Prayer:

Silent Contemplation (Meditation)

Psalm 46:10 (NIV): *"Be still and know that I am God; I will be exalted among the nations, I will be exalted in the earth."*

Silent contemplation involves quiet reflection on God's Word, presence, and will. It is a time of listening and waiting on God in silence.

Intercessory Prayer (Praying for Others)

1 Timothy 2:1 (NIV): *"I urge, then, first of all, that petitions, prayers, intercession, and thanksgiving be made for all people."*

Intercessory prayer involves praying on behalf of others, lifting their needs, concerns, and well-being to God.

Listening Prayer (Hearing God's Voice)

John 10:27 (NIV): *"My sheep listen to my voice; I know them, and they follow me."*

1 Samuel 3:10 (NIV): *"The Lord came and stood there, calling as at the other times, 'Samuel! Samuel!' Then Samuel said, 'Speak, for your servant is listening.'"*

Listening to prayer involves spending time in silence, seeking to hear God's voice, and discerning His guidance and direction in our lives.

These various forms of prayer can enhance your spiritual life and deepen your relationship with God as you engage with Him in diverse ways, expressing your love, repentance, gratitude, and dependence on Him.

Be Sincere and Authentic: Approach prayer with a genuine heart, being honest and open with God. Share your joys, concerns, doubts, and struggles. God desires a real relationship with you, so avoid holding back.

Psalm 62:8 (NIV): *"Trust in him at all times, you people; pour out your hearts to him, for God is our refuge."*

Matthew 6:6 (NIV): *"But when you pray, go into your room, close the door, and pray to your unseen Father. Then your father, who sees what is done in secret, will reward you."*

1 Peter 5:7 (NIV): *"Cast all your anxiety on him because he cares for you."*

Schedule and Develop a Prayer Routine: Create a consistent prayer routine that fits your lifestyle. Whether it is starting the day with prayer, praying before meals, or having a nightly prayer ritual, establish a regular practice that becomes an integral part of your day.

Psalm 55:17 (NIV): *"Evening, morning, and noon I cry out in distress, and he hears my voice."*

Acts 3:1 (NIV): *"One day Peter and John were going up to the temple at the time of prayer—at three in the afternoon."*

Psalm 119:164 (NIV): *"Seven times a day I praise you for your righteous laws."*

Keep a Prayer Journal: Consider keeping a prayer journal to record your conversations, prayers, thoughts, and experiences with God. This helps you reflect on the answered prayers, spiritual growth, and guidance received. It is a true blessing to go back and read what you prayed for and then see your requests come to fruition.

Psalm 77:11-12 (NIV): *"I will remember the deeds of the Lord; yes, I will remember your miracles of long ago. I will consider all your works and meditate on all your mighty deeds."*

Habakkuk 2:2 (NIV): *"Then the Lord replied: 'Write down the revelation and make it plain on tablets so that a herald may run with it.'"*

Psalm 119:15 (NIV): *"I meditate on your precepts and consider your ways."*

Seek Guidance from Scripture: Use the Word of God as a guide for your prayers. Seek wisdom, comfort, and direction from scripture. Find verses and passages that resonate with you and incorporate them into your prayers.

Psalm 119:105 (NIV): *"Your word is a lamp for my feet, a light on my path."*

Psalm 119:11 (NIV): *"I have hidden your word in my heart that I might not sin against you."*

Isaiah 55:11 (NIV): *"So is my word that goes out from my mouth: It will not return to me empty but will accomplish what I desire and achieve the purpose for which I sent it."*

Practice Gratitude in Prayer: Express gratitude to God for His love, blessings, and provision. Thank Him for His faithfulness and grace in your life. Take time to acknowledge His presence and faithfulness in your prayers.

Psalm 100:4 (NIV): *"Enter his gates with thanksgiving and his courts with praise; give thanks to him and praise his name."*

Colossians 3:17 (NIV): *"And whatever you do, whether in word or deed, do it all in the name of the Lord Jesus, giving thanks to God the Father through him."*

Psalm 136:26 (NIV): *"Give thanks to the God of heaven. His love endures forever."*

Ephesians 5:20 (NIV): *"Always giving thanks to God the Father for everything, in the name of our Lord Jesus Christ."*

Be Persistent and Patient: Remember that building a closer relationship with God through prayer is an ongoing journey. Be persistent and patient, knowing that God hears your prayers and will respond in His perfect timing and according to His divine plan.

Psalm 27:14 (NIV): *"Wait for the Lord; be strong and take heart and wait for the Lord."*

Proverbs 3:5-6 (NIV): *"Trust in the Lord with all your heart and lean not on your understanding; in all your ways submit to him, and he will make your paths straight."*

Psalm 37:7 (NIV): *"Be still before the Lord and wait patiently for him; do not fret when people succeed in their ways when they carry out their wicked schemes."*

By incorporating prayer into your daily life and making it a priority, you can develop a deeper connection with God. Prayer becomes a regular, authentic conversation through which you seek His presence, guidance, and strength. As you cultivate this practice, you will experience a closer relationship with God and a deeper understanding of His love and purpose for your life. Let us pray because prayer is important in bringing us closer to God!

My Story:

After being married for a few years, we moved into a nice suburban home. I was a resolute wife and a mother of four beautiful children. We attended church regularly and I studied the notes taken from Sunday worship, during the weekday. Despite the joy and satisfaction, I found by doing so, I sometimes felt overwhelmed and yearned for a deeper connection with God.

Aware of the challenges that came with my responsibilities of caring for young children and a working husband with a demanding career, I sought to find moments of stillness amid the chaos. As a result, I felt compelled to make a change to my daily routine and make a conscious effort to incorporate small intentional prayers to God throughout the day. I woke up a little earlier each morning, allowing myself precious moments of pure solitude before the demands of the day began.

I can still remember the sun peeking over the horizon, I settled into my favorite corner of the house, where a soft, cozy chair embraced my weary body. I was not a morning person by any means at that time, but I made an effort to wake up early and complete the task at hand. With my Bible in one hand and a journal in the other, I poured out my heart to God. Sharing my hopes, fears, and gratitude; I immersed myself in specific prayer.

I realized that my prayer time did not have to be confined to a certain posture or location but could extend throughout my day. As I moved about my household chores, nurturing, and caring for my children, I whispered prayers under my breath. Whether I was folding laundry or preparing meals, I found solace in conversing with my Heavenly Father.

Incorporating prayer into my daily routine transformed my entire perspective. Instead of viewing my tasks solely as burdens, I saw them as opportunities for communion with God. The simple acts of washing dishes became moments of gratitude and thankfulness for the provision of food. Helping my children with their homework became an opportunity to pray for their strength, growth, and wisdom. A hug to celebrate good grades and new learning, became an opportunity to pray and lay my hands on my children and ask for favor and protection over their lives.

I also realized the importance of involving my family in prayer. During family meals or before bedtime, I gathered my children and my husband (when I could), creating sacred spaces for prayer and thanksgiving. Sometimes, they would listen, repeat after me, or lead their own prayers. Together, they shared their joys and concerns, lifting them to God in unity. Sometimes, I can still hear their little voices in my head.

As this process continued, I witnessed remarkable changes. I found strength in times of exhaustion, peace amidst chaos, and guidance when faced with complex decisions. My relationship with God deepened, and I became more attuned to the gentle whispers of His voice. This to me was a gift awarded from Christ.

Incorporating prayer became a sanctuary during a busy life. It was a precious time of connection and vulnerability with the Creator, a lifeline that anchored my soul and nourished my spirit.

I discovered the transformative power of the ongoing conversations with God. It added a layer of intimacy to my relationship with Him, reminding me that He was not only a distant deity but a loving and forgiving Father who walked with me every step of the way. The intimacy I found in prayer permeated every aspect of my life, fulfilling me in a way I cannot describe with words.

It was evident that by incorporating prayer into my busy life as a young married woman with four children, had not only strengthened my relationship with God but also influenced my interactions with my family. I approached my role as a mother and wife with newfound grace and patience, extending love and compassion a little differently than I had in the past. The transformation was within me, through transformative prayer.

My children looked at me differently and responded to me differently as well. Soon after a while, they, too, began to cultivate their prayer habits. Prayer became the anchor that united our family, fostering open communication, and fostering a deeper faith in each of their hearts.

As years passed, my commitment to incorporating prayer remained steadfast. The difficulties of life became opportunities to seek God's guidance, find solace in His presence, and surrender my joys and struggles to Him. Through it all, my family grew closer to each other and God, guided by a mother who had discovered the profound impact of incorporating prayer into their everyday lives.

And so, my journey of incorporating prayer became a testament to the undeniable power of intimate communion with God. It was a reminder that, amidst the busyness and demands of life, prayer was the secret ingredient that infused their days with God's love and grace, as well as my own. Through the simple act of incorporating prayer into my life, I unlocked a deeper connection with God and set my family on a path of spiritual growth and unity. Another amazing gift from God for being obedient to Him.

Incorporating prayer had become a transformative practice that shaped our character, rooted our faith, and reminded us of God's constant presence. It was the lifeline that sustained us through trials, the source of wisdom in decision-making, and the catalyst for gratitude in every circumstance.

As my family and I continued our journey, we carried the lessons of incorporating prayer in our hearts, knowing that it was through this intimate and ongoing dialogue with God that our relationship with Him blossomed. We found comfort in knowing that our Heavenly Father was always listening, guiding, and pouring out His blessings upon our family.

Incorporating prayer has not only drawn us closer to God but also knit our hearts together as a family. We embraced each day, knowing that through prayer, they navigated life's joys and challenges with unwavering faith, love, and the assurance that we were never alone. May we all recognize the power of prayer and the transformative impact it can have on our lives, as we seek to draw closer to God and experience His abundant love and guidance.

The next step to drawing closer to God and building a close relationship with Him is through increasing your scripture study. We will discuss that in the next chapter so you can start taking deliberate steps to achieve it for yourself.

Your Story:

Chapter 3: Increase Scripture Study

Most of us are familiar with the verse from Joshua 1:8. "*This Book of the Law shall not depart from your mouth, but you shall meditate on it day and night, so that you may be careful to do according to all that is written in it. For then you will make your way prosperous, and then you will have success.*" It is extremely easy for the enemy to get in the way and get us distracted by the hustle and bustle of life. Just because we are busy with life does not mean we should let our guard down by not reading the word daily.

Part of the reason this has been put forth by the Psalmist in **Psalm 119:105:** "*Your word is a lamp to my feet and a light to my path*."

The word of God guides us throughout our Christian walk, just like the cloud and pillar of fire guided the Israelites in the desert during the day and night, as described in Exodus 13:21-22 (NIV): "*By day the Lord went ahead of them in a pillar of cloud to guide them on their way and by night in a pillar of fire to give them light so that they could travel by day or night. Neither the pillar of cloud by day nor the pillar of fire by night left its place in front of the people.*"

Isaiah 30:21 (NIV) goes further and shows just how studying the scripture moves us closer to God. "*Whether you turn to the right or the left, your ears will hear a voice behind you, saying, 'This is the way; walk in it.'*" This verse speaks of God's guidance, comparing it to a voice directing us on the right path.

Indeed, the Holy Bible emphasizes the importance of Scripture study and its role in deepening our understanding of God's word. Here are a few verses that highlight the value of studying and meditating on Scripture.

Psalm 119:11: *"I have stored up your word in my heart, that I might not sin against you."* This verse emphasizes the importance of internalizing God's word to guard against falling into sin. It provides armor against what is seen and not seen.

2 Timothy 3:16-17: *"All Scripture is breathed out by God and profitable for teaching, for reproof, for correction, and for training in righteousness, that the man of God may be complete, equipped for every good work."* This passage highlights the divine inspiration of Scripture and its ability to guide us believers in righteous living and prepare them for good works.

Romans 15:4: *"For whatever was written in former days was written for our instruction, that through endurance and the encouragement of the Scriptures we might have hope."* This verse underlines that Scripture offers instruction and encouragement, leading to hope and endurance through good and bad times in our lives.

Psalm 1:1-3: *"Blessed is the one who does not walk in step with the wicked or stand in the way that sinners take or sit in the company of mockers, but whose delight is in the law of the Lord, and who meditates on his Law Day and night. That person is like a tree planted by streams of water, which yields its fruit in season and whose leaf does not wither—whatever they do prospers."* The Scripture provides insight of endurance, power and strength gained by prayer. We become steadfast, steady, and strong in our position to love and trust God. We show our dedication to Him through prayer.

These verses, among many others, emphasize the importance of Scripture study in deepening our relationship with God. Regular study and meditation on the Word of God lead to spiritual growth, guidance, wisdom, and a firm foundation for righteous living. By immersing ourselves in Scripture, we believers gain a deeper understanding of God's will and are better equipped to follow His teachings in our daily lives. Studying to show ourselves approved is significant in deepening our relationship with God. The Holy Bible itself encourages believers to engage in the study and meditation of God's Word. Let's take a closer and more in depth look into the fruits of doing so.

Divine Revelation: Scripture is regarded as the inspired word of God, containing His wisdom, guidance, and revelations to humanity. Through scripture study, we gain insights into God's character, His plan of salvation, and His principles for righteous living.

This verse from 2 Timothy 3:16-17 emphasizes that all Scripture is divinely inspired and serves various purposes, including teaching us about God's character, correcting our understanding, and training us in righteousness. It highlights the comprehensive role of Scripture in equipping us believers for every decent work, which includes understanding God's plan of salvation and living following His principles.

2 Timothy 3:16-17 (NIV): *"All Scripture is God-breathed and is useful for teaching, rebuking, correcting and training in righteousness, so that the servant of God may be thoroughly equipped for every good work."*

Spiritual Nourishment: Just as physical nourishment is essential for the health of our bodies; spiritual nourishment is vital for the well-being of our souls. Scripture acts as spiritual food, providing sustenance for growth, inspiration, and renewal.

Jesus aptly put it in Matthew 4:4, where He describes the word of God as being essential for sustenance, indicating that just as physical food is necessary for physical life, spiritual sustenance from God's Word is essential for the life of the soul, providing growth, inspiration, and renewal. "Jesus answered, 'It is written: *"Man shall not live on bread alone, but on every word that comes from the mouth of God."*

Knowledge and Understanding: Through scripture study, as believers, we gain knowledge about God's nature, His will, and His purpose for humanity. It helps believers understand the teachings of Jesus, the examples of faithful individuals, and the principles that govern a godly life.

2 Peter 1:3 (NIV): *"His divine power has given us everything we need for a godly life through our knowledge of him who called us by his glory and goodness."*

Transformation and Guidance: Scripture has the power to transform hearts and minds, renewing and shaping individuals into the image of Christ. It guides making wise decisions, discerning truth from falsehood, and navigating the complexities of life.

Romans 12:2 (NIV): *"Do not conform to the pattern of this world but be transformed by the renewing of your mind. Then you will be able to assess and approve what God's will is—his good, pleasing, and perfect will."*

Spiritual Armor: Scripture is often described as a powerful weapon in spiritual warfare. Ephesians 6:17 declares that the Word of God is the "sword of the Spirit." By immersing ourselves in Scripture, we equip ourselves with spiritual armor, enabling us to combat temptations, overcome challenges, and stand firm in our faith.

1 John 4:9-10 (NIV): *"This is how God showed his love among us: He sent his one and only Son into the world that we might live through him. This is love: not that we loved God, but that he loved us and sent his Son as an atoning sacrifice for our sins."*

Discernment and Wisdom: Increased scripture study enhances our ability to discern truth from deception. It provides the foundation for wise decision-making, guiding us through the complexities of life. Psalm 119:105 states, *"Your word is a lamp to my feet and a light to my path."*

Spiritual Growth and Transformation: Scripture study helps us grow in faith, maturity, and spiritual transformation. As we meditate on God's Word Day and night (Psalm 1:2), it becomes a transformative force in our lives, aligning our thoughts, attitudes, and actions with God's will.

Studying scripture is one of the most important and rewarding activities that a Christian can do. The Bible is the word of God, and it reveals His character, His will, His plan, and His promises. The Bible also teaches us how to live a Godly life, how to worship God, how to pray, how to serve others, and how to deal with challenges and difficulties. The Bible is our successful guide to living a holy life.

But as we all know, studying the scripture is not always easy. It requires time, effort, discipline, and guidance. It also requires a humble and teachable attitude, a willingness to learn from others, and a desire to obey God's commands. I have found the following strategies help to increase scripture study.

1: Be part of a Bible study and be an active participant: Attend physical and virtual meetings and be an active member of the WhatsApp groups that focus on Bible study.

2: Use study guides: Bible study Bibles, concordances, commentaries, and various online resources will prove immensely helpful for you to understand the context, history, and interpretations of the scriptures.

3: Utilize technology: Do not just use the physical Bible; make use of Bible apps, websites, or digital versions of the scriptures to access various translations, audio versions, and study tools. The fact that there are diverse ways of consuming God's Word means you have no excuse for not studying the Word. You could play it on your drive to or from work or even the grocery store. You could even ask Alexa to play it for you in your house if you have any home automation tools.

4: Use AI in your Bible study: Yes, the famous ChatGPT is not just for passing college exams and writing marketing copies. You can incorporate it in your scripture study to make finding scriptures and explanations for different things easy for you. All you need to do is play around with different prompts to see how powerful it is.

For example – you can modify these prompts to find all manner of verses for about anything:
- "Find bible verses on {describe whatever you are looking for an explanation}."
- "Give me commentaries for the verse above."
- "Find more verses to support this."
- "What can I learn as a believer from all this?"

Take notes: You cannot afford not to take notes, whether you are in a group Bible study or a personal Bible study session. Take time to draw lessons from what you have learned and jot all of it down. Remember, writing down your thoughts makes it attainable.

Here are some principles that can help study the scripture effectively and fruitfully even as you apply all the hacks we have discussed.

Study the scripture with prayer.

Prayer is essential for studying the scripture because it helps us to communicate with God and to seek his guidance. Psalm 119:18 says, "*Open my eyes so that I may see wonderful things in your law.*" We need to ask God to open our spiritual eyes, minds, and hearts to understand and apply His word. We must also thank Him for His words and praise Him for His wisdom and grace.

Study the scripture with context.

Context is important when it comes to the study of Scripture because it helps us interpret the meaning and message of a passage. The context includes the text's historical, cultural, literary, and theological context. We need to consider the writer of the text, the time and place of writing, the audience, the purpose, and the relationship to other parts of the Scriptures. We must also compare Scripture with Scripture and use clear verses to explain ambiguities. This is the best way to truly declare God's promises in our lives during prayer. Think about it – quoting scripture out of context to God is very unlikely to yield the results you may be looking for.

Study the scripture with application.

Application is crucial for studying scripture. James 1:22 says, *"Do not merely listen to the word, and so deceive yourselves. Do what it says."* We need to not only hear and understand God's word but also obey and follow it. We need to ask ourselves what God wants us to learn from a passage, what He wants us to do or change, and how He wants us to grow in faith and love.

Implement what you learn.

The goal of scripture study is not just to gain knowledge but to change our lives as it is written in 2 Timothy 3:16-17. It says, *"All Scripture is God-breathed and is useful for teaching, rebuking, correcting and training in righteousness, so that the servant of God may be thoroughly equipped for every good work."*

As you study the scriptures, look for ways to implement what you learn in your daily actions and decisions. You can also write down your impressions and commitments in your journal or notebook. Implementing the scriptures can help you to grow closer to God and become more like Him.

Studying scripture is a lifelong journey that can enrich our relationship with God and transform our lives. Let us study the scripture with prayer, context, and application, and let us experience the power and the beauty of God's word.

Scripture analysis is a necessary part of our spiritual growth and progress. It assists us in discovering more about the divine being, His blueprint for us, and His directives. It also strengthens our belief, enhances our comprehension, and motivates us to live by His desires. As it says in 1 Peter 2:2, "*Like newborn babies, crave pure spiritual milk, so that by it you may grow up in your salvation.*"

Increasing Scripture study is essential for building a closer relationship with God. Through the Bible, we encounter the living Word of God and discover His wisdom, guidance, and love. Scripture study transforms our thoughts, actions, and perspective, helping us align our lives with God's will. It provides inspiration, comfort, and direction in our faith journey. By dedicating time to study, meditate, and apply the teachings of the Bible, we open ourselves to a deeper connection with God and experience the transformative power of His Word. May we all be encouraged to prioritize Scripture study and allow it to shape us into faithful followers of Christ.

My story summarizes much of what I have done to draw closer to God – you could use it to draw some lessons on how I have applied some of the information I have discussed in this chapter.

My Story:

I grew up in a Baptist household, attending church and vacation bible school from an early age. I accepted Jesus as my Lord and Savior, was baptized, and loved God. My foundation as a "babe in Christ" was established and growth was evident in my life. However, as I entered my early thirties, I found myself struggling to see a true pathway to a specific purpose God had for my life other than being a wife, mother, and loyal employee.

After feeling this way for a few weeks, I stumbled upon a Bible study group in my community, which was listed in our quarterly homeowners association newsletter. Intrigued by the idea or thought of meeting more women in my neighborhood, I decided to find out a little more about what was being offered. The group met every week, discussing different bible passages and exploring their meanings and applications. It took a few weeks to finalize my decision to attend but it finally happened, and I attended a session.

As I began to increase my Scripture study using a Bible just for women, I noticed a subtle change within myself. The more I engaged with God's Word, the more I discovered its timeless wisdom, guidance, and encouragement from a woman's perspective. I found solace in the Psalms during times of doubt and fear, strength in the narratives of David and Daniel, and inspiration in the teachings of Jesus. All of which had a deeper meaning that I had experienced in the past.

The weekly bible study helped me to see that the Bible is not just a book of ancient stories, but a living, relevant guide to everyday life. The verses I read started to shape my thoughts and actions, providing direction in decision-making and moral dilemmas. I found myself growing in faith and experiencing a deeper connection with God.

As I continued to increase my Scripture study, I realized the importance of consistency and discipline. I could see both men and women struggling, in the Bible and was able to align instances with specific challenges seen today in my life, the community, state, country and the world. The more I immersed myself in Scripture, the more I developed a hunger for knowledge and understanding. I sought out additional resources like commentaries, devotionals, and books that deepened my understanding of the biblical context and provided insights into the message of God's Word.

Furthermore, I discovered that Scripture study was not just an intellectual exercise but a transformative encounter with God. The Scriptures came alive with new meaning, and I felt a sense of awe and wonder as I discovered the depths of God's love, grace, and truth.

Through my increased Scripture study with other women in my neighborhood, I also found greater clarity and direction in my life. The truths I learned from the Bible guided my choices, transformed my character, and shaped my worldview. The accountability really helped me become more in tune with who God wanted me to be. I felt a stronger sense of purpose and a deeper love for God and others. To this day, I study and share scriptures with others; it makes me feel complete and useful to Christ.

As you study scripture, the next thing you should do is invoke Gratitude in everything you do.

Your Story:

Chapter 4: Invoke Gratitude

Psalms 107:1 clearly describes the life we should be living as Christians: "*Oh give thanks to the LORD, for he is good, for his steadfast love endures forever!*" This shows that God requires believers to practice thanksgiving in all circumstances.

Apostle Paul wrote in 1 Thessalonians 5:18, "*Give thanks in all circumstances; for this is God's will for you in Christ Jesus.*" This means that we should express our gratitude to God not only when things are going well, but also when we face trials, challenges, and difficulties. The key phrase here is 'In all circumstances." We can thank Him for His presence, His power, His wisdom, and His sovereignty **in every situation.**

Ephesians 5:20 emphasizes the same point of giving thanks: "*Always giving thanks to God the Father for everything, in the name of our Lord Jesus Christ.* "By recognizing and expressing gratitude to God, we always acknowledge His role, His provision, faithfulness, and blessings in our lives.

The Bible teaches us that gratitude should be a consistent and intentional practice that permeates all aspects of our lives. Specifically, Psalm 136:1-3 provides a beautiful example of gratitude: "*Give thanks to the LORD, for he is good, for his steadfast love endures forever. Give thanks to the God of gods, for his steadfast love endures forever. Give thanks to the Lord of lords, for his steadfast love endures forever.*"

This passage emphasizes the everlasting love and goodness of God, calling upon us to give thanks to Him. It reminds us that His steadfast love is constant throughout all circumstances and that gratitude should be an enduring response to His faithfulness.

Furthermore, Colossians 3:15-17 guides on living a life of gratitude, *"And let the peace of Christ rule in your hearts, to which indeed you were called in one body. And be thankful. Let the word of Christ dwell in you richly, teaching and admonishing one another in all wisdom, singing psalms and hymns and spiritual songs, with thankfulness in your hearts to God. And whatever you do, in word and deed, do everything in the name of the Lord Jesus, giving thanks to God the Father through him."*

These verses encourage us to let gratitude permeate our hearts and actions. Gratitude should extend far beyond mere words and manifest itself in our daily lives. It suggests that we allow the peace of Christ to rule in our hearts, filling us with thankfulness for His grace and guidance. The Word of God should dwell richly within us, prompting us to express gratitude to God through worship and teaching one another. In all that we do, gratitude should be the underlying attitude, as we recognize that everything we have and everything we are, is truly a gift from God.

Yes, gratitude should be an ongoing practice that extends into our thoughts, words, and deeds, enabling us to experience the joy and peace that come from a grateful heart. But how can we cultivate a grateful attitude in our daily lives? Well, the Bible provides the much-needed direction on how to go about this:

Start your day with a prayer of thanksgiving.

Psalm 118:24 guides all believers on how they can show their gratefulness each morning. It says, *"This is the day that the Lord has made; let us rejoice and be glad in it."* When we wake up in the morning, we MUST thank God for the gift of a new day, for His love and mercy, and His presence and guidance. We must also ask Him to help us be grateful for whatever He has in store for us throughout the day. We ask in knowing God hears our prayers and will grant the desires of our hearts.

Keep a gratitude journal.

Philippians 4:8 says, "*Finally, brothers and sisters, whatever is true, whatever is noble, whatever is right, whatever is pure, whatever is lovely, whatever is admirable — if anything is excellent or praiseworthy — think about such things.*" This verse is immensely powerful on its own. One way to practice this verse is to write down at least three things we are thankful for daily. Even if you can only list one thing to be grateful for, it is a great starting point. They can be big or small, simple, or complex, if they reflect God's goodness and grace in our lives, it is worth writing down.

Express your appreciation to others.

As believers, we are called to live in peace and harmony with one another; as Colossians 3:15 says, "*Let the peace of Christ rule in your hearts, since as members of one body you were called to peace. And be thankful.*" And one way to do that is to show gratitude to those who bless us in any way. We can say thank you, write a note, give a hug, or offer a compliment. We can also pray for others and ask God to bless them with or without their knowledge. Sometimes, the greatest gift to someone else is to show appreciation, kindness and love without public attention or acknowledgment. Some things can be done in secret and still be a blessing to others.

Share your blessings with others.

God has given us so much, and He wants us to share His gifts with others who are in need. 2 Corinthians 9:11 says, "*You will be enriched in every way so that you can be generous on every occasion, and through us, your generosity will result in thanksgiving to God.*" We can do this by giving our time, talents, money, or resources to help others who are struggling or suffering. We can also support a cause close to our hearts or join a ministry serving others in the name of Jesus.

Praise God for His works and His character.

As believers, we are required to praise God for who He is and what He has done for us. We can follow the example of the psalmist in Psalm 136:1 when he says, "*Give thanks to the Lord, for he is good. His love endures forever.*" He goes on to list many reasons why we should thank God, such as His creation, His deliverance, His protection, His provision, and His sovereignty. We can also sing songs of worship, read scriptures of praise, or join a community of believers who celebrate God's goodness and faithfulness. This too supports the importance of being with "like minded" individuals.

These are just some ways we can show gratitude using the teachings from the Bible. By doing so, we will not only honor God and bless others, but we will also experience more joy and peace in our hearts. This in itself is a gift from God.

My Story:

Contemplating the inception of starting a new company, I am overwhelmed with awe and thankfulness for the incredible manner in which God has steered and shown favor towards this venture. It commenced with a dream, a vision I wholeheartedly perceived as a divine ordination. This may be hard to believe in today's society, but God still speaks to us in our dreams.

One night I had a dream that I was up in the air on the left side of God. I could not see his face, but I could see He was with me. When I looked outward, all I could see were rooftops of homes, remarkably similar to a subdivision. God said to me, "These are your homes, and this is your land." I immediately woke up and told my husband about my dream. My husband replied, "Well, that's funny because we only have the house and land we live in now and the bank owns that." The very next night, I had the exact same dream. It was at that moment that I knew God was trying to tell me something about real estate, but that was all I knew.

The Bible is full of testimonies of God speaking to His people through dreams. *Matthew 2:13 "When they had gone, an angel of the Lord appeared to Joseph in a dream. "Get up," he said, "Take the child and his mother and escape to Egypt. Stay there until I tell you, for Herod is going to search for the child to kill him."* Such examples are given throughout the Bible to support what I experienced, as well as what many others may have experienced as well.

God had shown me the end result, yet did not provide the instructions on the what, when, where or how to accomplish the task. All I knew for sure was that I was the "who" within the equation and that God had a plan for me related to homes, land, and some form of real estate. A plan that I had not known of without His revelation to me in a dream.

Despite lacking prior experience in the field of real estate or construction. I embarked on this journey with complete faith. Completely confident that God would guide me at every turn, to fulfill what He had shown and told me in my dream. God led me on a path of placing the right people in the right places to provide expertise in areas

I lacked knowledge. Just thinking about it now gives me chills and places me in a mindset of sincere gratitude to God.

Though the path was strewn with obstacles and uncertainties, my steadfast trust in God's purpose for me to start my own company empowered me with resolve and fortitude like nothing I had experienced in the past. I had the privilege to observe the amazing and remarkable manifestations of divine intervention almost immediately. Throughout the process of establishing a new business, God orchestrated the arrival of the right individuals—advisors, mentors, and allies—who generously provided their wisdom and assistance. It became evident that God was orchestrating the elements of this endeavor, ensuring that I had the requisite guidance and aid to surmount the challenges that emerged along the way.

Although what I have shared does not include all the details of starting a new construction company, what I have included was the beginning of me making gratitude become an essential part of my daily routine. In moments of triumph and in times of struggle, I took time to pause and offer thanks to God for everything in my life. I recognized that every achievement and every setback were opportunities for growth and learning, drawing me closer to Him.

With passion and thanksgiving to God, the company flourished beyond my wildest dreams. The impact and success we experienced were not solely the result of our efforts but a testament to God's faithfulness and provision. My family was a huge part of what God had shared with me in starting a new company, especially my daughter Jasmine. A family business, the beginning of legacy, generational wealth and most importantly, a way for others to see God's glory, favor, and power in our lives.

In moments of doubt, I found solace in prayer, seeking wisdom and strength from God. I relied on His guidance to make crucial decisions, trusting that He would lead me in the right direction. And true to His promises, doors opened, opportunities arose, and the company continued to grow.

Witnessing the transformative power of God's hand in this journey deepened my faith and strengthened my relationship with

Him. It reminded me that with God, all things are possible, and He can use even the most unlikely individuals to accomplish His purposes.

As the company thrived, I made it a priority to share my gratitude with those around me. I encouraged my family to acknowledge and appreciate the blessings we received daily. Together, we celebrated milestones with humble hearts, recognizing that it was God who orchestrated our success.

Through it all, my heart overflowed with gratitude for the incredible privilege of being a vessel for God's work. I have seen firsthand how He can take a simple dream, fueled by faith, and turn it into a reality that impacts lives.

As I reflect on this remarkable journey of starting a new company with God's guidance, I am filled with awe and gratitude. It is a testament to the power of faith, trust, and obedience to God's word.

This experience has taught me that when we align our dreams and visions with God's will, He can accomplish far beyond what we could ever imagine through us, than what we can ever do by ourselves. It is important to remember that success is not just measured by financial gains or worldly achievements but by the impact we make and the lives we touch along the way.

In every step of this entrepreneurial adventure, God orchestrated divine connections, provided wisdom, and offered His unwavering support. He surrounded me with the right people, equipped me with the necessary skills, and opened doors of opportunity.

Gratitude became an integral part of my journey, reminding me to acknowledge and appreciate God's provision and faithfulness. It is through gratitude that I have found a deeper connection with God and a greater understanding of His love and grace.

I am humbled and blessed to have been a part of this incredible story. I hope that by sharing my experience, others may also be inspired to step out in faith, trusting that God's plan is far greater than anything we could ever imagine. To date, my story continues to evolve and expand to the next level of greatness.

With faith, passion, and gratitude, may we all embrace the dreams and visions God has placed in our hearts. Let us trust in His guidance, knowing that He will provide the resources, support, and opportunities we need to fulfill His purposes.

As we journey through life, may we continually invoke gratitude to God for every blessing, both big and small. Let us remember to give thanks for the challenges that strengthen us, the victories that shape us, and the people who walk alongside us. May our lives be a testament to God's faithfulness and grace. And may our relationships with Him grow deeper as we recognize His hand in every aspect of our existence.

In all things, let us strive to honor and glorify Him, knowing that through His infinite wisdom and love, we can accomplish extraordinary things. To God be the praise and the glory forevermore. Amen.

Your Story:

Chapter 5:
Inner Transformation

"Do not be conformed to this world, but be transformed by the renewal of your mind, that by evaluating you may discern what is the will of God, what is good and acceptable and perfect." **Romans 12:2.**

God wants us to be transformed when we know Him. We cannot be related to Him who is holy, righteous, and remain in sin. Just as 1 Peter 1:15-16 aptly puts it; *"But just as he who called you is holy, so be holy in all you do; for it is written: "Be holy, because I am holy."*

Inner transformation is the process of changing our thoughts, feelings, and actions to align with God's will and purpose for our lives. This is not something that happens overnight, but rather a lifelong journey of learning, growing, and renewing our minds in Christ. Inner transformation is essential to living a whole and fruitful Christian life because it enables us to overcome sin, resist temptation, love God and others, and fulfill our calling.

Romans 12:2 emphasizes the need for a renewed mind and transformation from the patterns and values of the world. The Holy Bible speaks extensively about the concept of inner transformation, highlighting its significance in the Christian faith. I have shared a few verses that underscore the importance of inner transformation:

2 Corinthians 3:18: "*And we all, with unveiled faces, beholding the glory of the Lord, are being transformed into the same image from one degree of glory to another. For this comes from the Lord who is the Spirit.*" This verse suggests that as believers behold the glory of the Lord, they are progressively transformed into His image, guided by the Holy Spirit.

Ephesians 4:22-24 also emphasizes the need to let go of our old sinful nature and be renewed in our minds, putting on the new self that reflects the likeness of God in righteousness and holiness. It says, "*Put off your old self, which belongs to your former manner of life and is corrupt through deceitful desires, and to be renewed in the spirit of your minds, and to put on the new self, created after the likeness of God in true righteousness and holiness.*"

It highlights the transformative power of God's grace and the ongoing process of becoming more like Christ.

As believers, we are encouraged to put on our new selves. As it is depicted in Colossians 3:10: "*and have put on the new self, which is being renewed in knowledge after the image of its creator.*" This new self, which is continually renewed in knowledge, is about conforming to the image of our Creator.

Galatians 5:22-23, says, "*But the fruit of the Spirit is love, joy, peace, forbearance, kindness, goodness, faithfulness, gentleness, and self-control. Against such things, there is no law.*" This verse highlights the transformation that occurs through the Holy Spirit's work in our lives, producing Godly virtues that exemplify Christ's character.

These verses, among others, affirm the Christian belief in the transformative power of God. They emphasize the need for inner renewal, the removal of old patterns and behaviors, and the growth of godly virtues through the work of the Holy Spirit.

Of course, this can only happen when we continuously subdue the flesh as directed in Galatians 5: 16-17 *"So I say, walk by the Spirit, and you will not gratify the desires of the flesh. For the flesh desires what is contrary to the Spirit, and the Spirit what is contrary to the flesh. They conflict with each other so that you are not to do whatever you want."*

Romans 8:5-6 also describes what is expected of us in this journey of transformation: *"Those who live according to the flesh have their minds set on what the flesh desires; but those who live by the Spirit have their minds set on what the Spirit desires. The mind governed by the flesh is death, but the mind governed by the Spirit is life and peace."*

Understanding the scriptures, how can we achieve inner transformation? Well, you must appreciate that this inner transformation is not a one-time event but an ongoing process that takes time. It involves surrendering ourselves to God, allowing Him to work in our hearts and minds, and conforming us to the likeness of Christ even when the spirit is willing, but the body is not.

As we yield to the transformative work of the Holy Spirit, we experience a deepening relationship with God and a gradual renewal of our thoughts, attitudes, and behaviors. Inner transformation is both a grace-driven journey and an active participation in cooperating with God's work in our lives.

As with the previous chapters, here are a few practical tips on how we can achieve inner transformation:

Recognize your need for inner transformation.

The first step to achieving inner transformation is to recognize your need for it. Romans 3:23 tells us that *"we are all sinners who fall short of God's glory"* and Jeremiah 17:9, says, *"Our hearts are deceitful above all things and desperately wicked."* We all have areas in our lives that need improvement, growth, or change. We all have sins, weaknesses, or traits that prevent us from living as God intended for us to live. We all have wounds, hurts, or fears that affect our relationships with God and others. We all have false beliefs, negative thoughts, or negative emotions that distort our minds and us as a whole.

However, that does not necessarily mean you have to live in sin as that will push you further from God. The Bible in Romans 12:2 tells us, *"Do not conform to the pattern of this world, but be transformed by the renewing of your mind..."* Therefore, we need to acknowledge our need for inner transformation and humble ourselves before God, asking Him to search our hearts and reveal anything that is not pleasing to Him as it is written in Psalm 139:23-24: *"Search me, God, and know my heart; test me and know my anxious thoughts. See if there is any offensive way in me and lead me in the way everlasting."*

Repent of your sins and receive God's forgiveness.

The second step to achieving inner transformation is to repent your sins and ask for God's forgiveness. Acts 3:19 tells all believers: *"Repent, then, and turn to God, so that your sins may be wiped out, that times of refreshing may come from the Lord."* Repentance means turning away from your sins and turning to God. It means confessing your sins to God and agreeing with Him that they are wrong.

And nothing makes the Lord happy like a sinner who repents their sins and seeks the Kingdom of God. This is evident in Luke 15:7 where it says, *"I tell you that in the same way, there will be more rejoicing in heaven over one sinner who repents than over ninety-nine righteous persons who do not need to repent."*

The Bible goes further ahead in 1 John 1:9 and tells us that *"If we confess our sins, he is faithful and just and will forgive us our sins and purify us from all unrighteousness."* It also tells us that if we repent, God will forgive our wickedness and remember our sins no more (Hebrews 8:12). Therefore, we need to repent our sins and receive God's forgiveness, which is freely available to us through the blood of Jesus Christ as it is written in Ephesians 1:7: *"In him, we* have redemption through his blood, the forgiveness of sins, by the riches of God's grace."

Renew your mind with God's Word.

The third step to achieving inner transformation is to renew your mind with God's Word. Renewing your mind means replacing your old thoughts, beliefs, and attitudes with God's thoughts, beliefs, and attitudes. It means meditating on, memorizing, studying, applying, and obeying God's Word. That means letting God's Word shape your worldview, values, goals, decisions, and actions.

The Bible tells us in Psalm 119:105: *"Your word is a lamp for my feet, a light on my path."* It goes further ahead in Hebrews 4:12 and says: *"For the word of God is alive and active. Sharper than any double-edged sword, it penetrates even to dividing soul and spirit, joints, and marrow; it judges the thoughts and attitudes of the heart."* Therefore, we need to renew our minds with God's Word, which can transform us from the inside out as it is guided by 2 Timothy 3:16-17: *"All Scripture is God-breathed and is useful for teaching, rebuking, correcting and training in righteousness, so that the servant of God may be thoroughly equipped for every good work."*

Rely on the Holy Spirit's power.

The Holy Spirit is the one who convicts us of our sins, guides us into all truth, and empowers us to live a Godly life. The Bible teaches us that we cannot achieve inner transformation by our efforts, but we need to rely on the Holy Spirit who lives in us. John 16:13-14 says, *"When the Spirit of truth comes, he will guide you into all the truth, for he will not speak on his authority, but whatever he hears he will speak, and he will declare to you the things that are to come. He will glorify me, for he will take what is mine and declare it to you."*

The Holy Spirit is the third person of the Trinity, who dwells in every believer and empowers them to live a godly life. It is only when we listen and follow the Holy Spirit that the Holy Spirit may help us hear from God and follow God's will and intended purpose. Romans 8:26-27 says, "*Likewise the Spirit helps us in our weakness. For we do not know what to pray for as we ought, but the Spirit himself intercedes for us with groanings too deep for words. And he who searches hearts knows what the mind of the Spirit is because the Spirit intercedes for the saints according to the will of God.*"

Apply God's word to your life.

Finally, to attain inner transformation, you need to apply God's word to your life. God's word is not only meant to be read, studied, and memorized but also to be obeyed, practiced, and lived. James 1:22-25 (NIV) says: "*Do not merely listen to the word, and so deceive yourselves. Do what it says. Anyone who listens to the word but does not do what it says is like someone who looks at his face in a mirror and, after looking at himself, goes away and immediately forgets what he looks like. But whoever looks intently into the perfect law that gives freedom and continues in it—not forgetting what they have heard but doing it—they will be blessed in what they do.*"

The Bible also tells us that God's Word is extremely useful for various purposes in our lives. As it is written in 2 Timothy 3:16-17 (NIV): "*All Scripture is God-breathed and is useful for teaching, rebuking, correcting and training in righteousness, so that the servant of God may be thoroughly equipped for every good work.*"

Colossians 3:16-17 (NIV): "*Let the message of Christ dwell among you richly as you teach and admonish one another with all wisdom through psalms, hymns, and songs from the Spirit, singing to God with gratitude in your hearts. And whatever you do, whether in word or deed, do it all in the name of the Lord Jesus, giving thanks to God the Father through him.*" This tells us that we should let God's word dwell in us richly as we share it with others. It also tells us that we should do everything in the name of Jesus and with thanksgiving to God.

Yes, of course, everything you read in this book will take you through an inner transformational journey. With that being said, please don't read this chapter in isolation but as a part of the big puzzle. The puzzle of drawing closer to God through applying what you learn from scripture, what you hear from God when He speaks or manifests in your life.

As a reminder, inner transformation is a continuous and steady process that requires discipline, perseverance, and the work of the Holy Spirit. It is a journey of exploration and learning, where you continually surrender to God's transformative power and actively cooperate with His work in your life. As you commit to this process of inner transformation, you will experience a deepening of your relationship with God, a greater sense of His presence, and a more profound understanding of His love and purpose for you.

My Story:

At one point in my life, I allowed friends to be a stronger influence on my decision-making than God, my husband or family. It is not a time that I am proud of, but a time in my life where I allowed myself to be misguided. For a while, I masked what was happening by identifying my feelings and actions as a mid-life crisis, but "it" was more than that. "It" was one unwise decision after another. A very confusing time in my life, and I feared the direction I was going. Trying to get back on track was not going to be easy; it was extremely hard to even fathom. However, I knew that something needed to change within myself; thus, a journey of inner transformation began.

I remember being alone in my room, closing my eyes and praying fervently, asking the Holy Spirit to work within me. I opened my heart to His guidance, ready to let go of old habits and attitudes that hindered my spiritual growth, and my time on this earth.

As days turned into weeks, I sought silence and stillness, allowing moments of introspection to reveal the areas in my life that needed transformation. At best, the process was painful to go through; I had to confront my weaknesses, insecurities, and selfish desires. But with every revelation, I offered them up to God, surrendering my will to His.

During this transformation, I immersed myself in Scripture, focusing on the Word of God like never before. Through the pages, I discovered His promises, His grace, and his unwavering love for me. The more I studied and meditated on His teachings, the more my heart aligned with His truth. It took a while, but I started to notice a shift within me. My perspective shifted from self-centeredness to compassion for others. I found myself reaching out to those in need, offering a helping hand, and spreading kindness wherever I went. The desires that once consumed me were replaced with a deep longing to fulfill God's purpose for my life.

As I continued this journey of inner transformation, I realized that drawing closer to God meant letting go of the notion of what I wanted or thought I needed and allow His Spirit to guide my steps. I embraced a spirit of humility, recognizing that I am a vessel in His hands and not of my own power.

Through this process of inner transformation, I have discovered a closeness to God that exceeds anything I had ever known before. In the stillness of my soul, I feel His presence, His peace, and His love surrounding me. My heart is filled with gratitude for the work He is doing within me.

In this journey of inner transformation, I have experienced the joy of knowing God more deeply and intimately. My relationship with Him is no longer distant or superficial but a genuine connection built on trust, love, and faith. The trials that once seemed insurmountable have become stepping stones toward growth and spiritual maturity. I have learned to rely on God's strength rather than my own, finding comfort in His presence even in the darkest of times.

Today, I continue to strive for transformation, knowing there are still areas of my life that need refinement. But I walk forward with confidence, knowing that God's grace is sufficient, and His power is made perfect in my weakness. I am reminded that this journey of inner transformation is not a destination but a lifelong pursuit. Each day offers new opportunities to gain experience closer to God, to reflect His love and grace, and to become more like Christ. With every step, I am grateful for His faithfulness and the joy of experiencing His transformative power in my life.

To anyone seeking a closer relationship with God, I encourage you to embark on your journey of inner transformation. It may not always be easy, but the rewards are immeasurable. Trust in God, seek Him wholeheartedly, and allow Him to mold you into the person He created you to be. You, too, can experience the triumph that comes from a transformed life in His presence.

Next, we will learn the need to integrate community in your walk.

Your Story:

Chapter 6: Integrate Community

Fellowship is an integral part of all Christian life. It is no wonder that the Bible in the book of Matthew 18:20 (NIV) says, *"For where two or three gather in my name, there am I with them."*

There are many benefits that we believers get from that and one of them is the fact that communing with others helps us believers stir each other up according to Hebrews 10:24-25 "*And let us consider how to stir up one another to love and good works, not neglecting to meet together, as is the habit of some, but encouraging one another, and all the more as you see the Day drawing near.*"

This verse emphasizes the importance of gathering with fellow believers, encouraging, and inspiring one another to love and good works. Note, the specific phrase "Integrate Community" may not be found in the Bible, the importance of community and fellowship among believers is highlighted throughout the Scriptures.

Romans 12:10-13: *"Be devoted to one another in love. Honor one another above yourselves. Never be lacking in zeal, but keep your spiritual fervor, serving the Lord. Be joyful in hope, patient in affliction, and faithful in prayer. Share with the Lord's people who are in need. Practice hospitality."* This passage encourages believers to be devoted to one another, serve one another, and practice hospitality, fostering a sense of community and mutual care.

Acts 2:42, 44-47: *"And they devoted themselves to the apostles' teaching and the fellowship, to the breaking of bread and the prayers. All the believers were together and had everything in common. They sold property and possessions to give to anyone who had a need. Every day they continued to meet in the temple courts. They broke bread in their homes and ate together with glad and sincere hearts, praising God and enjoying the favor of all the people."*

These verses from Acts 2 illustrate the early Christian community, where believers were devoted to one another, shared their possessions, met together, and worshiped God. It highlights the importance of community, sharing, and supporting one another, fostering a deep sense of fellowship and unity.

Psalm 133:1-3: *"How good and pleasant it is when God's people live together in unity! It is like precious oil poured on the head, running down on the beard, running down on Aaron's beard, down on the collar of his robe. It is as if the dew of Hermon were falling on Mount Zion. For there the Lord bestows his blessing, even life forevermore."*

This passage from Psalm 133 highlights the beauty and blessing of unity amongst God's people. When brethren come together in harmony and unity, it is likened to the anointing oil that consecrated Aaron as the high priest and to the refreshing dew on Mount Zion. The verse underscores the idea that God's presence and blessings are experienced in a distinct way when believers are in unity and fellowship with one another.

Again, the Bible may not use the specific phrase "Integrate Community," but these passages emphasize the significance of being part of a community of believers, actively engaging in fellowship, supporting one another, and growing together in faith. Building relationships within the community of believers is an essential aspect of a Christian's journey and can contribute to a closer relationship with God.

Below are examples of what you can do to integrate community and develop a closer relationship with God.

Find a Church or Spiritual Community

Finding a church or spiritual community that aligns with your beliefs and values can be a rewarding and fulfilling experience. However, it can also be challenging and daunting, especially if you are new to a place or unfamiliar with the options available.

Here are some steps you can take to find a church or spiritual community that suits your needs and preferences:

Pray and ask God for guidance and direction: The Bible says in James 1:5, "*If any of you lacks wisdom, you should ask God, who gives generously to all without finding fault, and it will be given to you.*" Being specific in your requests to God are essential to having an authentic relationship with Him. Finding a church or connecting to a spiritually positive group of believers is important. Therefore, it is equally important to ask God for what you want.

Do some research online or in person: Proverbs 15:22, says, "*Plans fail for lack of counsel, but with many advisers they succeed.*" Therefore, you can use websites, apps, social media, or directories to find churches or spiritual communities near you. You can also ask your friends, family, coworkers, or neighbors for recommendations or referrals.

Visit a few churches or spiritual communities that interest you: The Bible says in 1 Thessalonians 5:21, "*Test everything. Hold on to what is good.*" You can attend their services, events, or activities to get a feel for their culture, style, doctrine, and values. You can also talk to their leaders, members, or visitors to learn more about their vision, mission, and goals.

Evaluate your experience and decide what is best for you: Pray and seek God's confirmation and peace about your choice. Proverbs 3:5-6 NIV says, "*Trust in the Lord with all your heart and lean not on your understanding; in all your ways acknowledge him, and he will make your paths straight.*" You can compare the different churches or spiritual communities you visited based on your criteria and expectations.

You can also:

Join Small Groups or Bible Studies
One of the best approaches to growing in your faith and connecting with different believers is to join a small organization or Bible study. The small group normally consists of several believers who meet regularly to share their lives, pray, and observe God's Word. On the other hand, Bible study is more intense when it comes to the awareness of a specific Bible book or topic, normally facilitated by a counselor or leader. Both congregations allow you to strengthen your relationship with God and others and to apply the teachings of the Bible in your daily life. They provide you with a more intimate setting in which you get to speak about and explore spiritual subjects.

There are many benefits of joining a small group or a Bible study, such as:

Getting to experience authentic community and fellowship with other Christians. This is evident in the bible, particularly in Acts 2:42-47, which says "*They devoted themselves to the apostles' teaching and fellowship, to the breaking of bread and prayer... every day they continued to meet in the temple courts. They broke bread in their homes and ate together with glad and sincere hearts, Praising God and enjoying the favor of all the people. And the Lord added to their number daily those who were being saved."*

Proverbs 27:17: *"As iron sharpens iron, so one person sharpens another."* Therefore, when you join these groups, you can learn from each other's insights, questions, and experiences.

Receiving support, encouragement, and accountability from your group members. Galatians 6:2 says, *"Carry each other's burdens, and in this way, you will fulfill the law of Christ."*

In 1 Peter 4:10, believers are instructed, *"Each of you should use whatever gift you have received to serve others, as faithful stewards of God's grace in its various forms."* Therefore, with a group, you can discover and use your spiritual gifts to serve one another and the church.

Attend Worship Services Regularly

Consistently attending worship services allows you to connect with God in a communal setting. Engage fully in worship, participate in prayers and hymns, and listen attentively to the sermons which are engraved in Colossians 3:16, which says: "*Let the message of Christ dwell among you richly as you teach and admonish one another with all wisdom through psalms, hymns, and songs from the Spirit, singing to God with gratitude in your hearts.*" Being present and actively participating in the worship service helps cultivate a sense of belonging and enables you to receive spiritual nourishment and guidance.

Serve Others

Actively seek opportunities to serve others within your church community because serving others is one of the ways that we can show our love for God and our gratitude for His grace. This is particularly so because, in 1 Peter 4:10, we are told: "*Each of you should use whatever gift you have received to serve others, as faithful stewards of God's grace in its various forms.*"

Volunteer for various ministries, outreach programs, or charitable activities. By serving others, you not only follow the example of Jesus but also contribute to the well-being of your community. In Acts 20:35, Jesus himself said, "*It is more blessed to give than to receive.*" Serving allows you to build relationships, gain deeper insights into the needs of others, and experience the joy and fulfillment that comes from selfless acts of love.

My Story:

As I decided to take intentional steps towards building a closer relationship with God, one of the essential factors I discovered was the significance of integrating the community into my spiritual journey. It was through a beautiful experience that I truly comprehended the amazing power of building relationships with fellow believers.

One Sunday, I met with a group of sorority sisters in hopes of meeting kindred spirits on the same faith journey. As I entered the home of the host, a warm smile greeted me, instantly making me feel welcome. Have you ever heard the saying, "The first impression is the lasting impression"? Well, the first impression of being welcomed with like-minded women, made a positive impact on me. I began attending more social gatherings and events, eager to connect with others who are seeking a closer relationship with God.

However, it was during a small group study that the true power of integrating community truly came to life. Sitting among a diverse group of educated and successful women, we shared our joys, struggles, and personal encounters, with God and without God as the head of our lives. Listening to their stories and insights, I realized that we were not alone on this journey. We were united not only as sorority sisters but in our desire to draw nearer to God and grow in our sisterhood and faith.

Through these interactions, I witnessed the power of unity and support. We encouraged one another, prayed for each other's needs, as well as, provided accountability when necessary. It was within this community of sisterhood and love that I found solace, guidance, and genuine connections that deepened my understanding of God's love and favor on this earth.

The group shared not only their spiritual experiences but also their lives beyond the church and sorority meeting walls. We celebrated birthdays and milestones and even stood by each other during times of loss and hardship. The laughter, tears, and genuine care we experienced together showed me the power of true community and how it can strengthen our relationship with God.

As we immersed ourselves in various gatherings, study sessions, and outreach activities, the love of Christ flowed through every interaction. It was not just about attending events; it was about forming authentic friendships and being there for one another in times of need. These connections became a tangible reminder of God's presence in our lives. Through collective prayers, shared wisdom, and shared experiences, I gleaned insights and encouragement that would have been difficult to access in isolation. Hearing others' perspectives on Scripture and witnessing their manifestations of faith challenged and inspired me to seek a deeper relationship with God.

Integrating into this community of sisterhood also provided service opportunities. Together, we volunteered at local shelters, organized fundraisers for causes close to our hearts, and supported missions locally, as well as internationally. The collective impact we made as a unified body of believers, was a powerful testament to the love of Christ and our commitment to living out our faith.

In the process, I discovered that building a closer relationship with God was not just about my journey but also about the connections I made with others in the community along the way. Their presence, support, and shared experiences enriched my faith journey and reaffirmed the importance of integrating community into the pursuit of a closer relationship with God.

Through this sisterhood of community, I experienced the truth of Scripture in action, specifically the verse from Hebrews 10:24-25, *"And let us consider how to stir up one another to love and good works, not neglecting to meet together, as is the habit of some, but encouraging one another."*

As I reflect on this journey of integrating community into my spiritual growth, I am grateful for the friendships forged, the lessons learned, and the shared moments of sisterhood, worship, and service. These experiences have not only helped me grow closer to God but have also taught me the immeasurable value of walking together with other like-minded individuals on the path of faith.

Today, I continue to prioritize community and actively seek opportunities to connect with others who share the same desire to deepen their relationship with God. So much so, that I encouraged and supported my oldest daughter to be part of the sorority as well. She is my Legacy in more ways than one. I also long for my youngest daughter to one day have the same aspirations to continue the tradition, when the time comes. I have come to understand that it is not only my devotion and quiet moments of prayer that draw me closer to Him, but also the love, support, and unity found within a community of believers.

Together, we press on, encouraging one another and building each other up in faith as we journey toward a closer relationship with God. In the embrace of community, we find strength, encouragement, and the shared joy of experiencing God's love. As we continue to integrate community into our spiritual lives, we are reminded that we are not meant to walk this path alone but rather to walk alongside fellow believers, united in love and pursuit of a deeper connection with our Creator. Through our sisterhood, God speaks to and through us to encourage and spread the goodness of God.

Next, we will be learning about service, which is also one of my favorite ways to show compassion and love.

Your Story:

Chapter 7: Invest in Service

Matthew 20:28 aptly describes what Jesus came to do. *"Even as the Son of Man came not to be served but to serve, and to give his life as a ransom for many."*

This shows that even we believers MUST be ready to serve, just as Christ offered Himself to service. Jesus Himself exemplified the ultimate act of service by sacrificing His life for the redemption of humanity, according to Mark 10:45: "For even the Son of Man came not to be served but to serve, and to give his life as a ransom for many." Our goal is to be Christ-like! Jesus Himself came to serve others, setting an example for us to follow. Of course, we are not supposed to die for anyone's sins – Jesus already did that for us, as He was the gift to humanity from the Father. He played His role of dying on the cross for our sins.

Our roles are different in the body of Christ. All this is thanks to the gifts we have been bestowed with. We MUST serve God by using our gifts and abilities for the benefit of the Kingdom of God. Romans 12:4-5: *"For as in one body we have many members, and the members do not all have the same function, so we, though many, are one body in Christ, and individually members one of another."* Here, Paul emphasizes that as members of the body of

Christ, we all have distinct functions and gifts, and we are called to utilize them for the benefit of the whole body of Christ.

1 Peter 4:10 also talks about something similar; "*As each has received a gift, use it to serve others, as good stewards of God's varied grace.*" This verse emphasizes that each believer has received a unique gift or ability from God, and it should be used to serve others, taking care to be good stewards of the grace we have received.

Galatians 5:13 adds something else; "*For you were called to freedom, brothers. Only do not use your freedom as an opportunity for the flesh, but through love serve one another.*" This verse encourages believers to use their freedom in Christ as an opportunity to serve others selflessly and in love.

These verses highlight the biblical perspective on investing in service. By utilizing our gifts, talents, and resources to serve others, we not only fulfill the call to imitate Christ but also contribute to the well-being and growth of the community of believers. Service becomes an act of love, obedience, and a way to glorify God while spreading His message of hope and grace. But how can we invest in the service of God effectively and faithfully?

By seeking God's wisdom and counsel

Before you make any investment decision, reflect on the words in Proverbs 3:5-6 which say, "*Trust in the Lord with all your heart and lean not on your understanding; in all your ways acknowledge him, and he will make your paths straight.*" We should always seek God's wisdom and counsel through prayer, His word, and Godly advisers if we want them to come true because Proverbs 15:22 says, "*Plans fail for lack of counsel, but with many advisers, they succeed.*" Serve in areas and ways that are pleasing to you and glorify God. Your success on earth is a testament to what God has allowed.

By planning and being diligent

Proverbs 21:5 says, "*The plans of the diligent lead to profit as surely as haste leads to poverty.*" Investing in the service of God requires planning because when you fail to plan, you are planning to fail. Take financial and time commitments seriously with the intent to follow-through. It is easy to over commit, which lends to the importance of purposeful planning.

Also, we should not be lazy or wasteful with what God has entrusted to us but use it wisely and productively for His glory as guided by Proverbs 21:20, which says: "*The wise store up choice food and olive oil, but fools gulp theirs down.*" Be strategic and not try to be everywhere and everything to everyone. Be who God intended you to be by creating a legacy of service based on your God given talents. With social media only a click away, it is easy to get caught up in waiting to be everywhere and do everything we see others do. What God has for you is for you and no one else. Continue to become an expert in your craft of service, whatever that may be to help others and bring glory to God's Kingdom.

By being generous

Investing in the service of God also involves being generous with what we have. 2 Corinthians 9:6-7 says, "*Remember this: Whoever sows sparingly will also reap sparingly, and whoever sows generously will also reap generously. Each man should give what he has decided in his heart to give, not reluctantly or under compulsion, for God loves a cheerful giver.*" We should not be greedy or stingy with our resources but share them with those in need and support the work of the gospel. This means to ask God for a heart of generosity. When we give to others, we also give freely with faith; not knowing what our impact will be. Through faith be assured God will bless those who give without malice. Our joy comes from knowing no matter what the person does after generosity is given, our act of giving is pleasing to God.

By being faithful and trustworthy

Investing in the service of God also means being faithful and trustworthy with what He has given us. Matthew 25:14-30 tells the parable of the talents, in which a master entrusts his servants with a specific amount of money consistent with their skills. The servant who invested their money wisely and gained extra was praised by the master and rewarded with extra duties and pleasure. The servant who buried his money out of worry was rebuked by the master and punished. Jesus concludes the parable by saying, "*For everyone who has will be given more, and he will have an abundance. Whoever does not have, even what he has will be taken from him*" (Matthew 25:29).

This clearly shows that God expects us to do something with the gifts He has given us for His glory. Any and everything we currently have, are indeed gifts from God. We show our appreciation by sharing and being a blessing to others, symbolic of what God does for us each and every day. Serving is one of my favorite acts of kindness. The warm feeling I get from doing so is only a tiny peek of insight to what God feels when we have a heart of service. Let us make a commitment to serve others, which is supported time and time again throughout the Scriptures. Service is a form of worship, which is our next topic of learning and reflection.

My Story:

Over the years, I became known throughout town for my strength, leadership, and unwavering faith in God. I attended church and found solace in the teachings of the Bible. However, despite my strong faith, I felt a growing sense that I needed to do more to live out my Christian values.

One Sunday, my Pastor delivered a sermon on the concepts of servant leadership, drawing inspiration from the Bible and a book he had read. He spoke about the importance of putting others first, serving with humility, and leading by example. The message resonated deeply with me, and I felt a stirring in my heart.

I decided I wanted to become a servant leader with biblical intent. I began by volunteering my time and resources to various charitable organizations in my community and even other communities I felt needed assistance. I helped feed the hungry at a food pantry in an overpopulated area, visited the elderly in a nearby nursing home, and even started a free mentoring program for single mothers in need.

As I became more involved in these acts of service, my understanding of servant leadership deepened. I realized that being a servant leader wasn't just about helping those in need but also about listening, understanding, and uplifting the spirits of those served as well. I read passages from the Bible that reinforced these principals, including verses like *Philippians 2:3-4: "Do nothing out of selfish ambition or vain conceit. Rather, in humility, value others above yourselves, not looking to your interests but each of you to the interest of the others."*

My transformation extended beyond my volunteer work; it began to shape my daily life and interactions on a deeper level. I listened more attentively to friends, neighbors, and strangers, offering support and encouragement. I became known for my gentle wisdom and the kindness with which I treated those I met. My actions were not just out of obligation but flowed naturally from my heart for all to see.

Specifically, I remember a large new family moved into our neighborhood, struggling to adjust to their new surroundings. I heard about their challenges and decided to visit them. I spend hours talking with them, listening to their concerns, and offering advice, guidance, and support to their situation. My willingness to serve others with love and humility left a lasting impression on the newcomers, and within a few weeks, they were able to settle into the community more comfortably.

As time passed, my efforts continued and others began to follow my example, and the community flourished as a result. The new neighbors soon became pillars in the community and continued the tradition of welcoming those who moved in from other locations.

My journey to becoming a servant leader was not without challenges but brought about unwavering faith and dedication. I dealt with friends who showed envy and jealousy towards me, which was exceedingly difficult to understand. God helped me to realize that with great deeds also comes great responsibility. God was using me for His glory and none for myself. I learned the profound impact of what one person's commitment to serving others can have on an entire community.

My story served as a testament to the power of biblical principles and the transformative effect of a humble heart and servant's spirit. **Who I am today is because of service.**

The last step in building a closer relationship with God is igniting a spirit of worship.

Your Story:

Chapter 8: Ignite Worship

We are all called to worship as believers; "*Come, let us bow down in worship; let us kneel before the Lord our Maker.*" Psalm 95:6.

And there is a requirement for that:

"*...true worshipers will worship the Father in spirit and truth, for the Father is seeking such people to worship him. God is spirit, and those who worship him must worship in spirit and truth.*" John 4:23-24

Worship is the expression of our love, reverence, and gratitude to God, who is worthy of all praise. Worship is not only a personal act but also a communal one, as we join with other believers to honor God and proclaim His greatness. Worship is not limited to a specific time or place but can be done in any circumstance, with any attitude, and in any way that glorifies God. Examples are dance, song, theater, art and much more.

Every second of the day offers a unique opportunity to ignite worship and praise God. What makes the process special is the uniqueness each person on earth has to offer in the way each person thinks, feels, and demonstrates expression. In other words, no one can praise God "better" than anyone else. All forms of heartfelt praise are pleasing to God, in every way imaginable.

While the specific term "Ignite Worship" is not specifically mentioned as ignite worship, the Bible does emphasize the importance of fervent, joyful, and sincere worship. It encourages and supports believers in efforts to worship God with enthusiasm, passion, and awe, recognizing His greatness and majesty, such as in Psalm 95:6-7 where it says: *"Come, let us bow down in worship, let us kneel before the Lord our Maker; for he is our God and we are the people of his pasture, the flock under his care."* Additionally, the Bible highlights the role of the Holy Spirit in John 4:23 when it comes to igniting and guiding believers in their worship. It says, *"A time is coming and has now come when the true worshipers will worship the Father in the Spirit and truth, for they are the kind of worshipers the Father seeks."* God is waiting to hear and see the praise we have to offer. May His name be the sound of praise from our lips to God's ears! Amen.

Now let us explore some ways to ignite worship in service of God and how to use the Bible to support our worship. Also, we will look at some examples of worship in the Bible and how they can inspire us today.

Worship in spirit and truth.

Jesus said in John 4:23-24 (NIV): "...*God is spirit, and his worshipers must worship in spirit and truth.*"

To worship in spirit means to worship with our whole being, not just our outward actions or rituals. It means to worship with sincerity, passion, and devotion, not just with words or emotions. It means to worship with the guidance and empowerment of the Holy Spirit, who helps us to know God and to express our worship in ways that are pleasing to Him. It is engaging and truly heartfelt through and through. Communicating and connecting with God on the deepest level possible.

To worship in truth means to worship according to God's revelation of Himself in His word and His Son. It means to worship with understanding, faith, and obedience, not just with ignorance or tradition. It also means to worship honestly, with integrity, and authenticity, not just with hypocrisy or pretense. The truth comes from the Scripture and the connection comes from the heart. One must know that God is God in all his magnificence. The truth of God along with faith binds a connection which can only be spiritual.

Here are some Bible verses that can help us to worship in spirit and truth:

Psalm 51:17 (NIV): "*My sacrifice, O God, is a broken spirit; a broken and contrite heart you, God, will not despise.*" The feeling of despair and the unknown in life; God accepts us as we are and reassures us that He will not turn away. A beautiful example of the love God has for all.

Romans 12:1 (NIV): "*Therefore, I urge you, brothers and sisters, because of God's mercy, to offer your bodies as a living sacrifice, holy and pleasing to God—this is your true and proper worship.*" To literally give God all; a pouring out from the depths within. Giving all to God and leaving nothing behind for ourselves.

Ephesians 5:18-20 (NIV): "*Do not get drunk on wine, which leads to debauchery. Instead, be filled with the Spirit, speaking to one another with psalms, hymns, and songs from the Spirit. Sing and make music from your heart to the Lord, always giving thanks to God the Father for everything, in the name of our Lord Jesus Christ.*" The joy and love described by the scripture can be paralleled to the greatest expression of happiness and love possible. This type of joy and love can only be extracted from an authentic heart.

The examples from the Scriptures provide a foundation of belief and faith, along with being authentic and sincere in every way possible. Engaging with God on a level that is far more expressive than anything experienced towards another human being or living thing on this earth. So cherished, intimate, private, and confidential between you and God.

Worship with praise and thanksgiving.

Praise is the expression of our admiration and appreciation for who God is and what He has done. Thanksgiving is the expression of our gratitude and joy for what God has given us and how He has blessed us. Praise and thanksgiving are essential elements of worship, as they acknowledge God's greatness and goodness and inspire us to love Him even more. A special bond, with expressions of love through praise, thanksgiving, and worship.

Here are some Bible verses that can help us to worship with praise and thanksgiving:

Psalm 100:4 (NIV): "*Enter his gates with thanksgiving and his courts with praise; give thanks to him and praise his name.*" Happiness, glee, tears of joy and appreciation that comes from deep within is a great example of the outpouring of praise and thankfulness described in the Scripture. Have you ever experienced such joy? An amazing feeling of excitement that is above any experience imaginable on earth? Just thinking of entering the gates of heaven should be enough to bring an outcry of joy and celebration like no other. An allegiance to God through praise and thankfulness, Amen.

Psalm 150:6 (NIV): "*Let everything that has breath praise the Lord. Praise the Lord.*" Each second of life offers an opportunity to thank God for all that He has done, doing and will do in the future. Our sincere appreciation for all to the Lord. Praise is something we ask God to keep burning within us, forever more.

1 Thessalonians 5:16-18 (NIV): "*Rejoice always, pray continually, give thanks in all circumstances; for this is God's will for you in Christ Jesus.*" It is always easy to praise God in times of success and happiness. What about times of sorrow and pain? Times of chaos and uncertainty are part of life. We must find ways to hold on to the word of God and rejoice through it all, no matter what. God is our truest friend who cannot tell a lie and stands on His word forever. Just knowing God is constant in life constitutes praise of thanksgiving and joy, always.

Worship with music and songs.

Music and songs are powerful ways to express our worship of God. It can stir our emotions, engage our minds, and lift our spirits. Also, songs help to convey thoughts, feelings, and desires to God.

Music and song can unite us with other believers in harmony at times or even in fellowship, adding variety or creativity into worship.

Here are some Bible verses to help you worship with music and songs:

Psalm 33:3 (NIV): "*Sing to him a new song; play skillfully, and shout for joy.*"

Colossians 3:16 (NIV): "*Let the message of Christ dwell among you richly as you teach and admonish one another with all wisdom through psalms, hymns, and songs from the Spirit, singing to God with gratitude in your hearts.*"

Revelation 5:9-10 (NIV): "*And they sang a new song, saying:* "*You are worthy to take the scroll and to open its seals, because you were slain, and with your blood, you purchased for God persons from every tribe and language and people and nation. You have made them to be a kingdom and priests to serve our God, and they will reign on the earth.*"

Worship with service and obedience.

Service and obedience are practical expressions by which we manifest our worship toward God. Service is the outflow of love to others as we serve with gifts that God has given us for His purposes. Obedience is an expression of trust and submission to God's commands that He has issued. Both service and obedience please God since they speak about His character and glory.

Here are some Bible verses that can help us to worship with service and obedience:

Matthew 25:40 (NIV): "*The King will reply, 'Truly I tell you, whatever you did for one of the least of these brothers and sisters of mine, you did for me.'*"

John 14:15 (NIV): *"If you love me, keep my commands."*

Hebrews 13:15-16 (NIV): *"Through Jesus, therefore, let us continually offer to God a sacrifice of praise—the fruit of lips that openly profess his name. And do not forget to do good and to share with others, for with such sacrifices God is pleased."*

These are some ways to ignite worship in service of God and how to use the Bible verses to support our worship. Worship is not a duty or a ritual but a privilege. Worship is not a one-time event or a weekly activity but a lifestyle and a relationship. Worship is not about us or our preferences but about God and His glory. Let us worship God in spirit and truth, with praise and thanksgiving, with music and song, with service and obedience, and with all that we are and have. Amen.

Igniting worship is not just for ourselves but also for others. To be "fishers of men" is to tell the good news of our Lord and Savior, Jesus Christ. You and I are "fishers of men" who share the wisdom and discernment afforded by God. We are to tell the world through our actions, work, service to others and of course through praise, worship, and thankfulness. Allow yourself to be open to expressions of God's grace, mercy, and protection over our lives. Be an active participant in spreading the good news of Jesus Christ through testimonies of faith, day in and day out, to all who are ready to receive. Make praise part of your daily routine and watch your life change into a testimony to inspire others!

My Story:

For over 29 years, I dedicated my life to educating and nurturing students of all ages. It gave me immense joy to wake up each day to teach, mentor, guide, and lead campuses to excellence. Despite my passion for making a positive impact in the lives of others, the pressures within the public school setting often left me with a feeling of exhaustion with politics and lack of accountability. Prayer was part of my daily routine but more so general prayers to help me get through each work day. Yet, at times, I did not know if God heard my cry.

A turning point in my life came during a particularly challenging school year that I will never forget. Limited resources, budget cuts, personal agendas, and other outside influences made some days at work exceedingly difficult. I found myself arriving early and staying late, struggling to keep up with administrative tasks and keeping my focus on students as they deserved. Challenges with changes in the culture and community I served, pushed me to the limit and I leaned on God to get me through.

One evening, after a really tough day at work, I received a phone call that almost took my breath away. A beloved young man who attended my school had been hospitalized after being diagnosed with terminal cancer. The news was devastating to say the least and left me with a profound sense of helplessness. I spent the night in tears, silently crying out to God for this special young man, his family, and the entire school community. Little did I know at the time, I was experiencing burnout and the sad news made me feel like I had taken the last bit of unwelcome news that I could bear.

Desperate for comfort and relief, I remembered a conversation I had with a colleague about the power of worship. My colleague shared how worship provided peace through the worst of times when dealing with uncontrollable circumstances related to work. I remembered those words and took action. I went into my closet, shut the door, and turned on my favorite gospel playlist from my cell phone. At first, the words didn't move me at all; I just sat there looking into darkness. As the music continued, something inside of me began to shift. I cried and prayed for my student, his family, and the school.

When I returned to work the next day, I decided to do something different by praying before getting out of my car to walk into the building. I had already said a prayer and thanked God for waking me up that morning but did not include work. This time I was more intentional, very similar to the time I spent in my closet the evening before. When I finished praying, I felt a sense of calmness and had the energy to do my absolute best before walking into the school.

About 3 weeks into my new routine of praying, singing and praising God in my car before work, I was startled by an unexpected knock on my passenger window from a young lady I did not recognize. I pressed the window button to let the window down and asked how I could help. The young lady explained she did not mean to startle me but wanted to introduce herself. She did so by sharing she was the daughter of one of the custodians at the school. She went on to say that she was homeschooled and sat in her father's truck in the parking lot each morning until her mother was able to pick her up at 10:00 am. She said she had watched me for the past 3 weeks from the window of her father's truck, and wanted to know if I would teach her how to pray and love God just like me. The tears started to swell in my eyes and without warning I started crying uncontrollably. I had no idea anyone was watching me in the mornings; especially not a child of an employee.

After I calmed myself, I slowly opened my driver's side door and stepped out of the car. I gathered my things, closed the passenger window, and asked the young lady to come to me. When she walked around my car towards me, she immediately grabbed my waist and started to hug me. We embraced tightly without saying a word for some time before she asked me a question. "Would you pray with me?" she asked. I took a step back and our eyes connected. We held hands and I immediately began to pray. When I finished, we both said, Amen at the same time. She softly said, "God thank you for the Principal; she is good to the people here, Amen." We smiled at each other and wiped away our tears. She walked back to her father's truck and waved goodbye. I stood silently and watched the tinted window rise and close.

It was at that moment, I knew that God had provided a special opportunity for me to experience how to ignite worship. The fire within me, the burning passion of seeking God, the feeling of giving everything in me to God was amplified because I was not worshiping alone. I had someone with me, praying with me, seeking God at the very same time, and asking for the same things from God. He was pleased and I felt it through and through.

The entire experience helped me to realize that the connection with others had deepened my own faith in a way that I had never expected. This experience has stayed with me and helped me to understand the importance of worshiping with other believers who love Jesus Christ as their Lord and Savior just as much as I did. I had experienced how to ignite worship.

Your Story:

Conclusion

Building a closer relationship with God is more than the implementation of the 8 steps listed within this book; it is evidence that "The I's Have It" is a book for every reader. Eight steps, all beginning with the letter "I" to assist with developing a more intimate connection with God. It requires dedication, self-control, and a readiness to develop and acquire knowledge from His teachings and counsel. By adhering to these eight steps, you can start to experience His influence, tranquility, and strength. Do not forget that God cherishes you and desires a profound and private connection with you. He is always available, regardless of what circumstances you are in. The Lord is awaiting your move towards Him so He can move closer to you.

Introspection, Incorporate Prayer, Increase Scripture Study, Invoke Gratitude, Inner Transformation, Integrate Community, Invest in Service, and Ignite Worship; we have all experienced something close if not exact at various times in our lives. Each unique step allows insight into how to maximize the concepts on a personal level and apply new or refreshed learning to your own life. A summary of God's words, clarification, my stories, as well as your own are now all in one space. Revisit, rework, renew, pray, process, and proceed, as you move to the next level of your life with Christ.

The world was not designed for us to live throughout life alone. God has provided multiple opportunities for us to connect, build character, learn and to keep moving forward. God loves us from where we are right this minute. No judgment, shame, or reason to feel like you are alone. God is here, He is waiting on you to open the door and let Him in. Revelations 3:20 states, "Behold, I stand at the door and knock. If anyone hears my voice and opens the door, I will come in to him and eat with him, and he with me."

Share this news of this book with others you love, cherish or whom you feel would benefit from reading. It is an honor to have you read my book and I pray you have enjoyed all that it has to offer.

Congratulations!

A Prayer For You

Heavenly Father,

You have crafted the greatest book of all time. A guide for daily living, a source of answers for everyday trials, and most importantly, a route to get closer to You. The book "And The I's Have It" (Eight steps to building a closer relationship with God), is a creation of everything I need in one place to make amends, to make a change, to be in the best position possible to connect and hear from you. And because of You, "I" now have it!

The number eight is symbolic of a new beginning, new ways, new outlook and even a new life. The number eight is also a representation of making amends and the special fulfillment of Your purpose in my life. Please allow this book to take me on a journey to search deep within myself to analyze who I am right now (Introspection) before trying to add anything else on my plate. God, I thank you for the opportunity to admit who I am and know that through You, I can live with confidence of whom I belong. Living the life of a child of God.

I make time for what is important to me. You, God are important to me and through dedicated time to pray daily and consistently (Incorporate Prayer), I know my connection to you will only grow stronger. I now know the special formula of the perfect prayer is just to talk to You from my heart. Thank you in advance for listening and being a forever present help for me in times of joy and sorrow each moment of my life.

Learning to read the bible more purposely will provide a fulfillment of Your word within me like I have never known. Allow me dear God, to be taught through the interpretation and study of the bible (Increase Scripture Study). God, please allow the Scriptures to be a guide and roadmap for any questions I may have related to my life.

Soften my heart, mind, soul, and spirit to live daily with acknowledgement of You. Heavenly Father, please place in me an authentic appreciation, personal satisfaction, and thanksgiving (Invoke Gratitude) as only You can do. Allow me to be thankful like I have never been before. Thankful for all days and during all times; thankful without ceasing.

Change in me oh God, (Inner Transformation) anything that is not pleasing to you. Remove anything from the inside that does not reflect you on the outside. I pray that I represent you in my work, leisure, and praise for the world to see. Make my life an example of what You deem fit for others to see one of Your greatest works within me.

Surround and connect me with people who are chosen by you and are equally yoked (Integrate Community) dear God. Allow me to learn from others who believe, cherish, and have faith in you, that exceed our closeness and love. Allow me to be moved in a special and spiritual way to never lose the bond between my brothers and sisters in Christ.

Father, the act of love is service to others and the act of service to others is love. God, You have shown us the greatest act of service is love. You have designed a universe of opportunity to serve others. Instill and renew in me Oh God, a heart, mind, and spirit of service (Invest in Service). Keep me grounded to keep others before myself in service and truth.

Lord, my heart is open and longing for a deeper connection with You, in a unique way. I do not want to be lost in this life. Use me God, to make worship vibrant and full of life (Ignite Worship) truly reflecting my love for only You. Uproot me and use me to bring light to You in worship, praise, and song.

Right now, I surrender everything. All of me, anything in me, anything around me, anything above or below me, and even anything beside me, I surrender all. My life is not my own but is Yours. Thank you, thank you, thank you Jesus, for allowing me to truly be and live as a true child of God. My new life starts now. Jesus name I pray this prayer to You, **Amen.**

www.ingramcontent.com/pod-product-compliance
Lightning Source LLC
Chambersburg PA
CBHW071223160426
43196CB00012B/2403